EARTH CRAMMED WITH HEAVEN

A Spirituality of Everyday Life

ELIZABETH A. DREYER

PAULIST PRESS
NEW YORK • MAHWAH, NJ

Library of Congress Cataloging-in-Publication Data

Dreyer, Elizabeth, 1945-
    Earth crammed with heaven: a spirituality of everyday life/Elizabeth A. Dreyer.
        p.   cm.
    Includes bibliographical references and index.
    ISBN 0-8091-3450-0
    1. Spiritual life—Catholic Church. 2. Laity—Catholic Church, Religious life. 3. Catholic Church—Membership. I. Title.
BX2350.2.D74   1994
248.4'82—dc20   93-39808
                                                                            CIP

Published by Paulist Press
997 Macarthur Boulevard
Mahwah, NJ 07430

Printed and bound in the
United States of America

Table of Contents

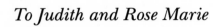

To Judith and Rose Marie

Acknowledgments

This book is the fruit of many years of reflection and dialogue with members of the faith community across the United States. People have been responsive and enthusiastic, allowing me to enhance and test my experience and perceptions with their own stories. These encounters with persons too numerous to name have been a privileged opportunity for which I am most grateful.

Periodically since 1984, I have also taught a course entitled "Spirituality of the Laity." It was in this classroom setting that literature, propositions, and perspectives on a spirituality of everyday life have been critically and systematically analyzed. I am grateful to all who participated in this process with insight and generosity. Their influence is present throughout this book.

Finally, I have tested my ideas with friends and family who struggle to live the kind of Christian life that is the subject of this volume. Among them are my sister, Virginia Navarro, and friends—Carolyn Beaudin, Toni Carroll, Judith Ford, and Rose Marie Conway. I am also grateful to the Washington Theological Union for a sabbatical leave, during which I wrote the final draft of the manuscript. Above all, I offer special thanks to my husband, John Bennett, whose remarkable editorial gifts helped me to hone a rather disparate group of ideas into a coherent whole. For his magnanimous love and support, I am ever grateful.

Earth's crammed with heaven,
And every common bush afire with God;
But only he who sees, takes off his shoes–
The rest sit round it and pluck blackberries,
And daub their natural faces unaware
More and more from the first similitude.
...

If a man could feel,
Not one day, in the artist's ecstasy,
But every day, feast, fast, or working-day,
The spiritual significance burn through
The hieroglyphic of material shows,
Henceforward he would pain the globe with wings,
And reverence fish and fowl, the bull, the tree,
And even his very body as a man....

Elizabeth Barrett Browning

Introduction

Even a cursory look at the history of Christianity shows
how infrequently the laity have succeeded in gaining and maintaining a place of importance and dignity in the church. Things
did not start out that way. In the nascent Christian community,
ministries were more diverse and activities such as teaching,
preaching, assisting the poor, celebrating the Lord's Supper,
choosing leaders and even hearing confessions and dying for
one's faith engaged a wide range of persons. During the intense
debates of some early church councils, educated laity, employed
as merchants and shoemakers, could be seen marching in the
streets, discussing and writing short treatises on theological
issues about which they felt strongly.[1]

But the role of the laity gradually diminished, and the
sense of the priesthood of all the faithful grounded in Christ
grew dim. Although there were periods and areas of notable lay
activity, over the years the loss of lay participation in church
affairs was real.

Today, once again, that participation is on the rise. In the
Roman Catholic Church one often hears the post-Vatican II
period described as the "age of the laity," and there is little
doubt that a fresh new breath of the Spirit is blowing in its
midst. But much work remains to be done as we sort through
how theologies of the Holy Spirit are influenced by the community's experience and, in turn, help to shape the ways in which
we find the Spirit present among us. Our theology directs us to
attend not only to our own situation, but to the spiritual renewal evident in many branches of the Christian church throughout
the world. The experiences of base ecclesial communities in
Latin America serve as a wellspring for liberation theologies,[2]

1

whose prophetic voices disturb and threaten our complacency. The forward-looking Dutch church is a model for the laity who seek to be full members in ecclesial decisions and functions. In a distinctive way, the laity are struggling to come into their own in North America as well.

One can reflect on this new awakening from several perspectives. First, Vatican II has affirmed the universal nature of the call to holiness based on baptism. "In the church not everyone marches along the same path; yet all are called to sanctity and have obtained an equal privilege of faith through the justice of God."[3] Must we not then question a church that continues to insist on sharp distinctions between clergy and laity and excludes laity from formal roles of power? Second, the stance of the church toward the world is changing dramatically. We no longer look upon the world with fear and suspicion, but acknowledge the many positive contributions of culture and human institutions. We struggle anew to establish links between the church and the wider social, political, economic community. We are not always sure how to forge these new ties and the transition often causes pain and confusion. But we sense that membership in the Christian community is intimately connected with our more primordial membership in the human community.

Third, the level of education, wealth and position of American Catholics has reached new heights. As a result, many lay Catholics now demand of their faith the same kind of maturity that they find in other aspects of life.[4] They are attending workshops, retreats, and reading the Bible and spiritual literature in record numbers. In the narrower confines of official church ministry, lay persons are engaged in the formal study of theology, acquiring credentials and taking their places in any number of ministries.

Given these developments, it is imperative that we continue to revise our understanding and practice of the spiritual life. The authority and responsibility for this task lies, not as it has in times past, in the hands of a few "officials," but with every baptized Christian. And the locus for such a spirituality lies not primarily in monastic and ecclesial dwellings, but in the homes, highways, and marketplaces of the world. This book is a contribution to the larger task of *aggiornamento* in the church. It calls for probing more deeply into the sacredness of our daily experience, taking the universal call to holiness with utmost seriousness, embracing a theology of creation, incarnation and Spirit, and critically appropriating the rich spiritual tradition upon which we stand. It is imperative that we continue to make thoughtful, integral connections between ordinary Christian life, in both its mundane and heroic moments, and what we as a faith community understand about holiness.

We are called to participate in the very life of God, a call that binds us to embrace freely the "way" of the saints in our own way, in our own time. This book aims to assist the community of believers in constructing a dwelling that is built on solid foundations, that welcomes everyone within and beyond the church to participate fully in the work of the Spirit and that empowers the entire People of God to become ever more attuned to the ways in which the world and their very lives reveal the human face of God.

NOTES

1. There is much historical evidence that lay involvement in the church and a high level of education go hand in hand. See Stephan Charles Neill and Hans-Reudi Webers, eds. *The Layman in Christian History* (Philadelphia: Westminster Press, 1963).

2. Liberation theology is most closely associated with Central and South America. This type of theology takes the experience of oppression as its starting point and invites ordinary persons to reflect on their life circumstances in the light of the gospel and then to act to bring about liberation. Major authors include Juan Luis Segundo, Gustavo Gutierrez, Ada Isasi-Diaz, Elsa Tamez, and Leonardo Boff.

3. *Constitution on the Church*, II.33.

4. See Joann Wolski Conn, *Spirituality and Personal Maturity* (New York: Paulist Press, 1989).

PART I
FOUNDATIONS FOR A
SPIRITUALITY OF
EVERYDAY LIFE

Part I is theoretical grounding for Part II. It examines the experiential, methodological, historical and theological foundations for a spirituality of everyday life. It advocates an informed, intelligent and authentic appropriation of our spiritual lives. Chapter 1 describes and orders the meaning of the term "spirituality," and identifies the laity in terms of their role in history. The goal of chapter 2 is to return the spiritual life to those who live it, encouraging a more mature, responsible attitude toward one's own call to holiness. It also asks why we should speak about a specifically "lay" spirituality. Chapter 3 argues for the importance of a critical and creative appropriation of the tradition, one that draws upon its strengths and sets aside its inadequacies. Chapter 4 examines three recent trends in theology that support a spirituality of everyday life—the Spirit, creation and incarnation.

1

What Is Spirituality? Who Are the Laity? And Why Is Everybody Always Talking About Them?

I. WHAT IS SPIRITUALITY?

"...The common practice of resorting to such terms as spirituality in order to hide ignorance or mask incoherence or disguise a void immeasurably increases and complicates the inherent vagueness of the language of spirituality."[1] How does one go about heeding this perceptive warning of William Stringfellow? The topic of spirituality is certainly in vogue, as a glance at the religious section of any bookstore confirms. Stringfellow elaborates on the confusion:

> "Spirituality" may indicate stoic attitudes, occult phenomena, the practice of so-called mind control, yoga discipline, escapist fantasies, interior journeys, an appreciation of Eastern religions, multifarious pietistic exercises, superstitious imaginations, intensive journals, dynamic muscle tension, assorted dietary regimens, meditation, jogging cults, monastic rigors, mortification of the flesh, wilderness sojourns, political resistance, contemplation, abstinence, hospitality, a vocation of poverty, nonviolence, silence, the efforts of prayer, obedience, generosity, exhibiting stigmata, entering solitude, or, I suppose, among these and many other things, squatting on top of a pillar.[2]

Stringfellow's point is not to deny that God can be present

7

in such multifarious activities, but rather to draw our attention to the potential in spirituality for exploitation and self-deception. As with most trends, the spirituality movement is attended by the weaknesses and pitfalls of a fad, as well as by the genuine excitement, searching, and promise of a way to understand, name and live a deeper relationship with self, others, world and God. To engage in the latter is a challenging task indeed. Stringfellow's warning should always be before us, a reminder to keep us honest and spur us on to clarity of thinking and expression.

This book considers the broadening understanding of spirituality since Vatican II.[3] Earlier, we would have understood the term "spirituality" to refer primarily to prayer. Then, with Vatican II the concept began to encompass one's entire faith life. Now we struggle to connect spirituality with all of life, not just its explicit faith dimension. Special attention is being given to neglected aspects of life such as the body, the emotions and matter. Some see the spiritual life in sociopolitical terms, emphasizing the struggle for justice. The term now also reflects ecumenical concerns and is used by other branches of Christianity and indeed, by members of other world religions. One hears about feminist spirituality, Black spirituality, Hispanic spirituality and even Marxist spirituality![4] Indeed, we argue in chapter 11 that spirituality needs to take the entire cosmos into account. Overall, spirituality refers to one's fundamental religious orientation to others, work and recreation, society, and nature.

Specific definitions and descriptions of spirituality are legion.[5] We can benefit by inquiring how leading theologians and historians define the term in its broadest dimensions. Ewert Cousins offers a very inclusive definition of spirituality in his preface to the series, *World Spirituality*. His formulation transcends the specificity of individual world religions. Since some traditions do not speak of the divine, he focuses the definition on the human person:

> The series focuses on that inner dimension of the person called by certain traditions "the spirit." This spiritual core is the deepest center of the person. It is here that the per-

son is open to the transcendent dimension; it is here that the person experiences ultimate reality. The series explores the discovery of this core, the dynamics of its development, and its journey to the ultimate goal. It deals with prayer, spiritual direction, the various maps of the spiritual journey, and the methods of advancement in the spiritual ascent.[6]

Although the initial perspective is anthropological, the human core of which it speaks is understood as the place where the human meets the transcendent. The third sentence is quite broad in scope, whereas the final element narrows the focus to elements that are overtly religious, e.g., prayer, spiritual direction and methods of growth.

In this same series, Arthur Green, editor of the volumes on Judaism, describes Jewish spirituality as: "Seeing the face of God, striving to live in His presence and to fashion the life of holiness appropriate to God's presence."[7] In Part II, we reflect on the concrete building blocks of a spirituality of everyday life in quite similar ways, inviting the reader to see the human face of God in the daily round of activities.

Although one can identify common elements present in the spiritualities of many of the world's religions, one also detects important differences in emphasis. For example, Islam stresses inwardness and the real and abiding, as opposed to the transient nature of things. Hindu spirituality highlights the experience of "turning around" or conversion from the world to God. It advocates a sense of detachment from the world—not to be understood as unconcern, but as freedom from entanglement in anything that falls short of ultimate reality. Appreciation for the Christian "way" can only be enhanced as one becomes aware of the rich spiritual traditions of our Muslim and Jewish and Confucian brothers and sisters around the globe.

Three Perspectives

In the midst of this breadth and diversity, what can we say to establish some order and common ground? One can look at spirituality from three perspectives.[8] First, one can speak of what might be called the originating experience of God. At some specific point in history, a person falls in love with God. In many ways, the actual contours and nuances of this experience are very personal, intimate and defy adequate description. One has only to call to mind what it is like to fall in love to understand the ineffable quality of such an experience. Because ordinary language proves inadequate, the world has been filled with poetry, art, music and dance—modes of expression that usually do a better job at conveying the power of being in love.

Access to such experiences is also difficult, even when the person is a family member or a close friend. We can never quite "get inside" the experience of another, although its fruits are often visible exteriorly. Time also intervenes to complicate the task. How much more difficult it is to discern the religious experience of Origen, who lived in the second century, of Augustine in the fourth, or of Teresa of Avila in the sixteenth. In these cases, not only is the experience hard to penetrate, but one must also consider cultural milieux, self-understandings, and theological categories distant from, and foreign to, our own. But however inaccessible the entirety of such experience is, it is imperative that we keep this "falling in love" before us. It is the source, the energy, the moving force behind the expressions that often flow from the original experience.

Second, the originating experience of God usually takes shape in a variety of religious expressions. Many lovers of God record their experiences, leaving for posterity a written account of their love affair and what it meant to them. Examples of such "classic" texts include Augustine's *Confessions*, Gregory of Nyssa's *Life of Moses*, Julian of Norwich's *Shewings*, Luther's hymns and *Catechisms*, Francis de Sales' *Introduction to the Devout Life*, John Woolman's *Journal*, Etty Hillesum's *An Interrupted Life*, Dag Hammarskjold's *Markings*, and Dorothy Day's *The Long Loneliness*. These texts have been tested through the ages by their ability to instruct, to move, and to spur to action subsequent generations of God-seekers.

Quite often these experiences of falling in love with God have resulted in a written rule of life. Some of these rules are quite fluid and general, others explicit and elaborately wrought. Examples include the sayings of the desert fathers and mothers as well as the rules of groups such as the Benedictines, Carmelites, Cistercians, Franciscans, Dominicans, Augustinians and Jesuits. In the modern period, rules of life continued to emerge, e.g., the Salesians, Daughters of Charity, Missionary Servants, Sisters of Mercy, Sisters of Notre Dame, Sisters of St. Joseph. These documents formulate teachings about the lived experience of God and are aimed at guiding and preserving a way of life that flows out of, and is in continuity with, the founder`s originating experience.

Indeed, the actual lives of these communities seem to be an extension of the founder's experience of God. We have histories of the activities of these communities—activities that embody in a concrete and tangible way the original inspiration of the founder. In addition to communal living and prayer, such groups engage in service to the poor, healing ministries, education, and contemplation. Each community struggles to live out its particular charism which is often tied to the history, personality, and distinctive gifts of the founders and earliest members.

Finally, we can also think about spirituality in terms of scholarly reflection, analysis, interpretation and organization of the experiences, texts, and activities spoken of above. A great deal of this formal study revolves around the written texts that are extant, simply because they are concrete expressions readily available to us. However, the study of religious experience extends beyond these texts to the lives and practices of those who have sought to live out their encounter with God in their daily lives. The laity have begun to assume their rightful place in this reflection.

Scholars rely on many disciplines to assist them in their task. The tools of those who study spirituality now include anthropology, history, psychology, sociology, literary analysis, ecology and even economics. The academic discipline of spirituality, because it looks at experience from the perspective of the widest possible horizon of ultimate reality, is necessarily interdisciplinary.[9]

Even though students of spirituality have access to a wealth of data, it is well to remember the millions of "holy ones" who left no records, who founded no communities, who are anonymous and historically invisible. It would be a mistake to think that the experiences of famous spiritual ancestors like Pseudo-Dionysius, Bonaventure, Hadewijch of Antwerp, Meister Eckhart, Catherine of Siena or Elizabeth of the Trinity were radically discontinuous with ordinary folks in their own time or with those in ours. All of these persons lived as members of society, were often deeply affected by it, certainly contributed to it, and were influenced by the trends, ideas, affections, crises and glories of their day. And the legacies of such persons continue to reverberate with the experience of those who read them in subsequent eras. But knowing that we have never even heard of the majority of saints helps us maintain a healthy circumspection in our task. Because of this, we must be slow to make apodictic proclamations about the spiritual life. We remember that God's ways are not our ways and that God works in mysterious and hidden ways. The very presence in our own lives of outstanding holy ones who will not be known or remembered by the wider community, serves as a daily reminder of the breadth and depth of God's graceful presence in the world.

While these attempts to delineate and clarify our understanding of spirituality are necessary and helpful, they must always be considered in the context of one's own experience, understanding and desires. A true spiritual journey is not lived vicariously, but only by getting on the road ourselves and testing the terrain. There is no substitute.

II. WHO ARE THE LAITY?

In 1959, Yves Congar began his long and careful work on the laity with the observation that the word *laikos,* whence our "lay," is not found anywhere in the Bible.[10] In the New Testament, the noun *laos* is, however, used frequently and often carries the meaning, "people." In the Hebrew scriptures, the comparable term usually designates the "People of God" in opposition to the gentiles. For the Hebrew and early Christian communities these terms embraced an aspect of sacredness—those who were in relationship with God—and stood in contradistinction to those outside the covenant.

The term "laity" was also used to distinguish the wider community of the People of God from its leaders—priests, levites and prophets. The laity was that part of the church subject to the leadership and control of the hierarchy.[11] In the first half of the second century, in a letter to the community at Corinth (xl, 5), Clement of Rome distinguishes between the "special place" and "special ministries" of the priests and the lay people who are "bound by rules laid down for the laity."[12]

The division between clergy and laity took shape during the second and third centuries. Peter Brown refers to the rise to dominance of rabbis within Judaism and the strict division between clergy and laity in Christianity as "two silent revolutions that would determine the future development of religion in Europe and the Near East." He goes on: "What made the history of the Christian Church notably different from that of other religious groups was the constant anxiety of its clergy to define their own position against the principal benefactors of the Christian community," that is, the laity.[13]

It is this later meaning that has remained prominent and that today we are struggling to overcome. It is not difficult to uncover statements that insult or denigrate the laity. An oft-quoted example from the nineteenth century is the statement of Cardinal Gasquet: "The lay person kneels before the altar, sits below the pulpit—and puts his hand in his purse."[14] Then there is Monsignor Talbot's response to Newman's position on consulting the laity in doctrinal matters:

> What is the province of the laity? To hunt, to shoot, to entertain. These matters they understand, but to meddle with ecclesiastical matters they have no right at all, and this affair of Newman is a matter purely ecclesiastical...Dr. Newman is the most dangerous man in England and you will see that he will make use of the laity against your Grace.[15]

This is not to say that the laity have never been well regarded in the history of the church. Although few in number, there have been statements that point to and extol the variety of roles in the church.[16] The twelfth chapter of Paul's first letter to the

Corinthians is by far the most familiar. "Now there are varieties of gifts, but the same Spirit; and there are varieties of service, but the same Lord; and there are varieties of working, but it is the same God who inspires them all in every one" (1Cor 12:4–6). A second example comes from a bishop whose office led him to appreciate the broad and diverse charisms of the church. Ambrose of Milan (d.397) refers to Acts 6 and the need for the diversity of functions in the church. He observes that although the apostles leave off table service to engage in prayer and listening to the word, it is Stephen, chosen to serve at table who is filled with the Holy Spirit.[17]

Although histories of the church usually have little to say about the laity, we do know about some of their ecclesial activity.[18] As part of the recovery of the universal call to holiness, it is important for the laity to trace those parts of their history that are available in order for them to take their rightful place in the church today. A few examples follow.

After Constantine established Christianity as the religion of the empire in the fourth century, lay emperors and kings often assumed responsibility for the religious welfare of the people, representing the laity at synods and councils. In addition to their role as king (*rex*), they also assumed some of the responsibilities associated with priesthood (*sacerdos*). Another lay group were merchants who travelled widely to do business, and saw themselves as missionaries, bringing Christianity to the foreign lands they visited.

During the Middle Ages, many lay Christians participated in the Crusades. By joining in these military movements to recapture the Holy Land, the laity atoned for sin, helped to insure their salvation, and found a channel for the intense religious fervor of this period. And one must not overlook the role of religious leadership undertaken in families, especially by women. While the stories of most women are lost, we do know about the martyrs Perpetua and Felicitas; Macrina, the sister of Basil of Caesarea and Gregory of Nyssa; women who went to the desert to follow a life of prayer and penance; Augustine's mother, Monica and the lives of many devout royal women.

In the sixteenth century, the Reformation tried to redress the imbalance between laity and clergy by making the Bible, liturgy and catechetical material available in the vernacular. Later centuries saw continuing lay involvement in ecclesial architecture, religious literature and music; in liturgical renewal, devotional and retreat movements and Catholic action. The nineteenth century witnessed a strong stand for the laity taken by John Henry Newman in England and by Orestes A. Brownson and Isaac Hecker in the United States.[19]

Many lay movements, from the desert mothers and fathers to the medieval mendicant and Beguine movements,[20] arose in a spirit of reform, calling the church to simplicity, singleness of purpose and a prayerful life, providing a channel for intense religious feeling of ordinary persons. But too often the spiritual energy of these lay movements was unable to be sustained. Some groups lost a sense of direction and order, threatening the stability of the church. Sometimes the confusion was due to a lack of leadership and healthy incorporation into the church. Sometimes movements attracted marginal persons who were ill-equipped to live up to the standards originally envisioned. But in other instances, church leaders found such movements threatening and worked to control them by bringing them into already existing church structures. This often resulted in effectively blocking the new work of the Spirit in the community.

More recently, in a review of two books on the laity from Britain, one can read:

> Our age should bring to the church "Mr. and Mrs. Saints," "Saints William and Mary" or "Henry and Alice," lawyer saints etc. Lay saints will not be the result of ill-fitting or "trickle down" clerical spirituality.[21]

And lastly, although there are many elements in his book that need updating, Congar says in *Lay People in the Church:* "...if the Church, secure on her foundations, boldly throws herself open to lay activity, she will experience such a springtime as we cannot imagine."[22]

Movements toward change are needed at all levels and joint effort from a variety of perspectives can do much to move the church toward a more constructive idea of the laity. It is clear that the Spirit is moving in a distinctive way today in the lay community, and the search for a more meaningful spirituality presses forward with intensity at this juncture in history. We can be grateful for significant advances since Vatican II. The emphasis on openness and dialogue with all aspects of our human existence is bound to have a positive influence on lay spirituality. *The Pastoral Constitution on the Church in the Modern World* highlights Christian solidarity with all peoples and articulates an incarnational theology that closely links being religious with the fullness of our humanity.[23] But the image of the laity as "helper" with overtones of subordination perdures.[24] Happily, this image is no longer central in our documents, but it may remain in the minds of many lay persons and too often, in the spoken and unspoken atmosphere of our churches.[25]

Conclusion

The realization that we have held narrow and grossly inadequate concepts of the spiritual life is a challenge to the entire church to engage in sustained change. While there is much to be gained from the tradition, there is also need for creative thinking that will incorporate the lay experience into the larger arena of the church's spiritual life. How do we, as laity, understand prayer, contemplation, virtue, work? What is our attitude toward the body, toward sexuality, toward the material world? How do these things figure in the spiritual journey? Our most valuable resource in this area is the experience of lay persons who are paying attention to the ways in which God is present in their daily lives.

We must talk about lay spirituality at the present time, while also looking forward to a time when this would no longer be necessary. The ultimate goal remains clear: to reverence every member of the body in his or her unique dignity as a creature of God and to affirm the universal invitation to participate in the fullness of the divine mystery. We need to find out from each other how God works in our lives, and to shape our language and concepts about the spiritual life in response to open, respectful, *mutual* communication. God will call whom God wills and the Spirit will blow freely if we but allow it.

Holiness is judged, not by office, sex or prosperity, but by its fruits. Love, justice, peace, joy, patience—fruits that are present in many lives, irrespective of lifestyle, occupation or role in the church.

NOTES

1. William Stringfellow, *The Politics of Spirituality* (Philadelphia: The Westminster Press, 1984), p. 16.

2. Ibid., p. 19.

3. See Sandra Schneiders, "Theology and Spirituality: Strangers, Rivals, or Partners?" *Horizons* 13/2 (1986): 253–274.

4. Ibid., pp. 254–255.

5. See, e.g., Philip Sheldrake, *Spirituality and History* (New York: Crossroad, 1992), pp.32–65. See also Joann Wolski Conn, ed., *Women's Spirituality* (New York: Paulist Press, 1986), pp.1–30 and 49–58. Joann Conn: "Christian spirituality involves the human capacity of self-transcending knowledge, love, and commitment as it is actualized through the experience of God, in Jesus, the Christ, by the gift of the Spirit." *Women's Spirituality,* p. 3. Anne Carr describes spirituality as "the whole of our deepest religious beliefs, convictions, and patterns of thought, emotion, and behavior in respect to what is ultimate, to God." Ibid., p. 49.

6. Ewert Cousins, "Preface to the Series," in Bernard McGinn and John Meyendorff, eds., *Christian Spirituality I: Origins to the Twelfth Century* (New York: Crossroad Publishing Company, 1985), p. xiii.

7. Arthur Green, "Introduction," in Arthur Green ed., *Jewish Spirituality I: From the Bible through the Middle Ages* (New York: Crossroad Publishing Company, 1986), pp. xiii–xiv.

8. In this section, I am indebted to Walter Principe, s.v. "Spirituality, Christian" in the *New Dictionary of Catholic Spirituality* (Collegeville, MN: Liturgical Press, 1993).

9. See Sandra Schneiders, "Theology and Spirituality: Strangers, Rivals, or Partners?" *Horizons* 13/2(1986): 253–274.

10. *Lay People in the Church: A Study for a Theology of Laity* (London: Geoffrey Chapman, 1959), p. 1.

11. Edward Schillebeeckx, *The Layman in the Church* (New York: St. Paul Publications, 1963), pp. 35–36.

12. The Epistles of St. Clement of Rome and St. Ignatius of

Antioch, trans. James A. Kleist (London: Longmans, Green & Co., 1961), p. 34.

13. Peter Brown, *The Body and Society* (New York: Columbia University Press, 1988), pp. 142, 144.

14. Cited in the introduction by John Coulson, *On Consulting the Faithful in Matters of Doctrine* by John Henry Newman (New York: Sheed & Ward, 1961), p. 17.

15. Ibid., p. 41.

16. I would draw an analogy here to the feminist movement today. One can document movements toward equality for women throughout history, but never have they worked their way into the fabric of society in such a way that equality becomes the rule and oppression the exception. It is such long-standing and deeply rooted mores that are so difficult to turn around.

17. *Exposition of the Gospel of Luke,* VII, 86. *Sources chrétiennes* 52, 1958, p. 37.

18. One of the rare scholarly studies on the history of the laity is *The Layman in Christian History,* eds. Stephn Neill and Hans-Ruedi Weber (Philadelphia: Westminster Press, 1963). Unfortunately this valuable volume is out of print.

19. Joseph P. Chinnici gives a sense of the American Catholic laity from 1860–1900 in *Devotion to the Holy Spirit, in American Catholicism* (New York: Paulist Press, 1985), pp. 3–90. See also his *Living Stones: The History and Structure of Catholic Spiritual Life in the U.S.* (New York: Macmillan, 1988); Patrick Carey, ed., *American Catholic Religious Thought* (New York: Paulist Press, 1987); Lawrence Cunningham, *The Catholic Heritage* (New York: Crossroad, 1983); George Gallup Jr. and Jim Castelli, *The American Catholic People: Their Beliefs, Practices and Values* (Garden City, NY: Doubleday, 1987).

20. "Beguines" is the name given to a late medieval lay women's movement that was centered in the Low Countries. "Beghards" refers to a similar lay spiritual movement of men. See Ernest McDonnell, *The Beguines and Beghards in Medieval Culture* (New Brunswick, NJ: Rutgers University Press, 1954).

21. *The Layman in the Church* by Michael de la Bedoyere (Chicago: Henry Regnery Co., 1955) and *We Are Men* by John M. Todd (London: Sheed & Ward, 1955), reviewed by D.J.G. *Worship* 10(November 1955), p. 591.

22. *Lay People in the Church,* p. xxx.

23. *Pastoral Constitution on the Church in the Modern World,* Preface 1; Introduction. 11.

24. *Decree on the Apostolate of Lay People,* Chapter II.6.

25. As recently as thirty years ago, in an article, "Is There A 'Lay Spirituality?'", C.A. Bouman answers negatively, the reason for his answer resting in his assumption that the spirituality of religious life is normative for all and needs merely to be adapted to those living "in the world." He is certainly correct in identifying the primary elements of the spiritual life as common, namely the glorification of God and the imitation of Christ. What is problematic is his focus on the vows as the superior, more radical means to these ends. In this interpretation the quality of radicality is determined by lifestyle (lay/religious) rather than, by purity of heart and heroic love. *Worship* 27(May 1953): 279–286.

2

Whose Life Is It Anyway?

I. MEANING AND EXPERIENCE

Traditionally, the laity have had a minimal role in determining the meaning of the spiritual life. Because of a history in which the lay community was not expected to be "expert" on spiritual and theological issues, the locus of authority remained almost exclusively within clerical hands. As a result, the lay community has not acquired the necessary knowledge and skills that would have enabled them to influence how the church understands spirituality. A second consequence of this history has been a widespread lack of confidence about naming God and about interpreting life in spiritual terms. The laity have been expected "to pay and obey" and to take direction from the "authorities" on spiritual things. And they have! An additional factor in the laity's disenfranchisement was a narrow understanding of grace. Access to grace, whether through the Bible, the sacraments, or other means, was tightly controlled by the clergy.

Fortunately, recent theological "turns" have led to a reexamination of the sources of meaning, and the laity are beginning to reclaim their rightful role in naming new ways to understand the spiritual life. Theology has always been concerned with religious meaning. Meaning takes shape in feelings, symbols and language. Meanings also have histories. As we have noted, the history of the term "spirituality" included the wider lay community only in a marginal sense. But meanings do change as the community's experience changes, thus shaping and altering past meanings.

More often than not, reality has been understood in terms of two antithetical poles—subjective and objective. Objectivity was "something-out-there" that was reliable, rational and true.

Subjectivity was personal, probably clouded by feeling, unreliable and not to be trusted. Men were seen to have an edge on objectivity and were therefore better equipped to run society. Women were more subjective and therefore not to be trusted with "important" matters.

Today we are both the inheritors of, and participants in the gradual breakdown of, this subject-object dichotomy. The Canadian Jesuit, Bernard Lonergan, has made a major contribution toward this breakdown. He describes objectivity as true subjectivity, bringing the two intimately together.[1]

Meaning, Lonergan contends, emerges out of the authentic reflection of a community of persons, and does not drop full-blown from the sky like a *deus ex machina*. Naming one's world both orders that world and allows us to orient ourselves within it.[2] Naming, in a sense, creates reality, shaping it in deliberate, intentional ways. One characteristic of powerlessness is the inability to participate in the naming of the world. As the laity attend to their daily experiences of God, they need to articulate that experience so that the church's understanding of spirituality can be enriched and made more inclusive.

Things come to mean one thing or another as a result of a long and complex process of events, ideas, and interaction among persons. This holds true for spiritual values as well. It is now essential to ask *who* assigns meaning to spiritual realities; where and when the meaning was determined; and whether the inherited meaning continues to make sense to each of us in our own time, bringing with it energy and a renewed commitment to the gospel. The responsiblity of the lay community to participate in this process of assigning meaning in the realm of spirituality has never been greater.

Experience

This perspective on meaning necessarily places experience at the heart of things, in creative tension with inherited tradition. In terms of the spiritual life, this perspective calls for a new ownership by all the baptized of their daily experience as well as a critical appropriation of the past. The laity cannot accept without thought what has been handed down from past generations.

Rather, they must pay reverent attention to daily existence as the locus and seedbed for the ongoing revelation of God.

A hallmark of contemporary theology is its reliance on experience. A theology out of touch with human life is a theology that is arcane and empty. Karl Rahner's theology makes new radical claims about the intrinsic connections between human experience and the ultimate Mystery we call God.[3] The human drive to endless questioning and reaching out to ever wider horizons ultimately opens us out to God, making our connection with God an essential aspect of our being. The depth dimensions of living continually reveal God to us—in our loving, our integrity, our courage, our willingness to forgive and to act justly for the world. An incarnational theology overturns two-track schemas in which one's religious existence and the daily round of living run forever in parallel, never-to-meet lines.

Expressions of the two-track schema are easy to find. For some who find themselves in the throes of a powerful conversion, explicit religious experience becomes the only "real" experience and they bide their time between retreats or Bible study. Job, family and society become unwelcome interruptions in one's "religious" life. Others see their everyday lives of work and family as "real life," while church and religion constitute a valuable, but basically separate reality. But when one begins to consider daily experience as the primary locus of God's presence, such a dichotomy no longer makes sense. One must then begin to search for a new paradigm, a new way to make ultimate sense of life in its totality.

We are called to pay renewed attention to daily life, to see, hear, touch, smell and speak with a new awareness. This attention is supported by the conviction that one will meet God in the ordinary as well as in the extraordinary. We need to be on the lookout for the word of God in the world, a word that may be spoken in unlikely places, in experiences of simple joy and success as well as of hardship and suffering.[4]

Since theology emerges out of the experience of the community, we must articulate the full spectrum of that experience. We need to correct past exclusions by including the voices of the silent ones—women, persons of color, the laity. A task of the laity, then, is to attend to experience, to reflect on that experience in light of the gospel and to speak about the ways in which God is present or absent, comforting or challenging.

As we examine the "meaning-making" task in terms of religious experience, we realize that we do not stand alone. As Christians we are the inheritors of a rich tradition. We are blessed with God's creation, our family traditions, the church, the local worshipping community, angels, saints, mentors, relationships of all kinds. But in the last analysis, as a member of these many communities, the individual must decide about the meaning of the many aspects of his or her spiritual life. In a profound way, our intentionality is a key ingredient determining whether we notice God everywhere or only in church or only in suffering, or nowhere. It all depends on how we choose to fashion our world.

Of course, the risk of error is always with us. As humans, we are a combination of glory, holiness, freedom, and egotism, bias, sin. The most illustrious among us—those to whom we look as models of holiness—have always been acutely aware of this truth. But our penchant for getting it wrong cannot excuse us from the responsiblity of naming our world. From the earliest days of the church, this assignment of meaning has been going on. The earliest Christians who heard stories and had personal experiences of Jesus, interpreted these stories, attached meaning to them and wrote them down. This process has never ceased and while imperfect, it calls us again and again to trust in the Spirit's presence in each individual and in the community and to risk the adventure.

Given these developments, there is a good deal of discussion at the present time about how exactly we should understand the various aspects of church life—spirituality among them. Would it be more advantageous to deemphasize the different groups in the church—cleric, religious, lay—or should we, in fact, be attending more carefully to their respective distinctions? Let us examine this question.

II. WHY SHOULD WE SPEAK ABOUT A "LAY" SPIRITUALITY?

To the question of whether it is helpful and productive at this point in history to speak about a specifically lay spirituality, there are conflicting answers with substantive arguments on both sides. However, any acceptable answer has to address both the lack of visibility of the laity in the history of spirituality and the impact of a radically incarnational theology on our understanding of the spiritual life. If we don't emphasize lay spirituality, it is doubtful whether we can overcome this lack, or discover both the identity and role of the lay saint in the church.

Calling special attention to the neglected elements that distinguish the lay vocation from that of clergy and vowed religious can begin to identify and dignify the spiritual lives of all the members in the community.

Opposing Arguments

One argument against acknowledging and developing a lay spirituality centers on the fear of continuing harmful divisions we have known in the past. Having separate spiritualities can emphasize differences at the cost of commonalities, and give play to the human penchant to label one as better than the other. Some lay persons even feel that using the term "lay spirituality" calls attention to the church's neglect of the laity in the past—a past that they would like to leave behind. But, in general, this position holds that singling out any group is harmful and inevitably makes other groups feel excluded. And if speaking of a lay spirituality makes others feel excluded, it should be avoided—even if spiritualities in the past have excluded lay persons. The gospel message is inclusive and is not served by exchanging one kind of exclusivism for another.

This view also questions the ways we often distinguish religious/cleric and lay. Chief among these distinctions is the laity's position "in the world." But in addition to a newfound positive regard for "the world," it is increasingly difficult to understand how priests and religious are not "in the world." In some cases, members of these groups are "in the world" up to their eyeballs—one thinks of soup kitchens and involvements in Central America—and even the small number in cloistered, contemplative situations are often intimately linked up with "the world." Thomas Merton is an obvious example.

Second, some say that because it is impossible to account for the enormous diversity in the lay community, we should give up the enterprise altogether. In monasticism, one can more easily take stock of differences since they often arrange themselves in distinctive charismatic patterns. We can identify the spiritualities of Dominicans, Franciscans, Carmelites, Augustinians, Basilians, Jesuits, and others.

A third alternative is to redefine the meaning of terms such as "priest" and "laity," returning to an earlier tradition. In the biblical understanding of the "people," the priest is "taken from among the people"—not in the sense of being separated from them, but of being closely akin to them. In the letter to the Hebrews, Jesus' priesthood reveals how closely he is united with us and therefore able to understand our plight. In this way, we could say that the lay state underlies every position in the church—clerics, religious and laity—each performing different functions in the church. In this scenario, all spirituality would be primarily lay spirituality.

A related approach also points to the universality of the lay vocation. Everyone spends at least a quarter of her or his life as a lay person, and even if a religious or clerical vocation is chosen later, the roots of one's spirituality and value system go back to a lay milieu in the family. This perspective sees lay spirituality as the primary foundation for everyone.

A final argument against a specifically lay spirituality is based on the conviction that there is only one gospel and therefore only one Christian spirituality. It further emphasizes those basic elements applicable to all persons, regardless of state in life, sex, or even denominational affiliation. This argument states that differences in lifestyle are relevant, but not central to discussions on the spiritual life. Proponents opt to minimize these differences in order to focus on those things shared by all groups in the church. Persons who hold this stance argue that if our aim is unity of all persons in Christ, then talk about "lay" spirituality can only serve to divide rather than unite the community.

After all, elements of the spiritual life shared by all persons include self-knowledge as an important starting point for the spiritual life; desire for God; nurturing one's relationship with God through prayer; awareness of sin; practice of virtue; and love of neighbor. Anyone undertaking a journey toward holiness must attend to these issues, thus eliminating the need for a specifically lay (or clerical, or religious) spirituality. In his letter to the Galatians (3:27–29), Paul gives us a glimpse of the life of all those baptized and clothed in Christ. Distinctions between Jew and Greek, slave and free, male and female recede before the vision of unity in Christ Jesus.

Having examined some of the grounds for a negative answer to the question, "Should we speak about a distinctively lay spirituality?" let us move on to look at the arguments for an affirmative answer to the question.

In the Affirmative

It is not difficult to establish that in the history of Christian spirituality, the meaning and use of the term "laity" have often had pejorative connotations. As we have seen, the term "laity" has not always been used just to distinguish a specific group in the church, but has often carried with it meanings of "less," "inferior," "second-class." The laity have been thought incapable of attaining the fullness of the spiritual life, or by simple omission have not figured at all in discussions of spirituality. The rise of monasticism, the lack of education in the larger community, and the emphasis in the church on hierarchical structures, all contributed to a situation in which those writing about the spiritual life were almost exclusively religious and clerics, giving the impression that theirs was the primary and normative forum for discussions about the spiritual journey.

These negative aspects of the hierarchical structure of the church create the need to speak about a lay spirituality. To the extent that the church's hierarchical organization has been used for so long to exclude and to imply the inferiority of a group in the church, to that extent does the excluded group need a specific articulation of its spiritual way in order to maintain its identity and affirm its significance. A quick glance at the list of canonized saints reveals the problem in a dramatic way. Those in power in the church have, by and large, held up members of their own group for recognition and emulation as models of holiness. Male, clerical celibates dominate the official roll of saints, masking the saintly lives lived in the broader community.

Given these historical realities—the neglect and denigration of the laity—one must admit that talk about lay spirituality is one legitimate way to correct past abuses and is therefore urgently needed. Some have opted to adapt spiritualities originally intended for monks or nuns for the laity,[5] but much more needs to be done, not the least of which is a rethinking of the very anthropological and theological foundations upon which spirituality rests. This is the aim of this book.

A second reason for an affirmative answer has to do with the church's relationship to culture. A vibrant spirituality is one that is in tune with, and therefore able to speak to, the culture in which it finds itself. This harmony does not deny the radical gospel criticism of destructive elements in our society, but if one's understanding of the spiritual quest is divorced from the daily round of life's activities, neither a vital spirituality nor a prophetic stance for justice can prosper.[6] The result of such a split is a kind of schizophrenia. The spiritual life becomes artificial, a pseudo-life or something added on to "real life." When a church as an institution becomes significantly removed from the culture of which it is a part, it atrophies, takes on an air of unreality and eventually is unable to speak in a meaningful way to its people. At this moment in history, we can celebrate the newfound vibrancy in the lay community, a new life that is instrumental in reconnecting religious experience with the larger society. As always, the test of spiritual vibrancy lies in the community's ability and willingness to do justice, love kindness and walk humbly with God (Micah 6:8).

A third consideration argues for the need for specific structures supportive of lay spiritual life. This need has existed throughout the tradition. In the fourteenth century, partly in reaction to scholasticism and to the exclusive use of Latin, spiritual works became available in the vernacular, making them more accessible to the lay community. Resistance to this democratization of the spiritual life culminated in the Inquisition and in prohibitions that tried to keep the Bible and spiritual works out of the hands of "idiots" and "emotional women." Thus the church did not provide adequate support and education for the wider faith community. In his book, *Unquiet Souls,* Richard Kieckhefer suggests that some of the shortcomings in the life and writings of Margery Kempe may have been due to the difficulties of trying to live a saintly life without the support of a monastic structure. The laity needed comparable structures that could provide education, support and the means to continue development in the spiritual life.

> The more religious the urban laity became, and the more it imitated monastic piety, the more difficult it would be to distinguish lay from clerical or religious mentality. The dilemma was how to reconcile monastic ideals with lay existence.[7]

The lack of creative imagination on the one hand, and resistance by authorities on the other, have prevented a full flowering of spirituality for the laity—a serious loss to the spiritual health and vibrancy of the church.

Today, where ecclesial decisions and statements about the meaning of holiness do not include full representation, voice and vote of the lay community, this pattern continues to the detriment of all. As more laity identify the need for ongoing spiritual growth and seek for ways to become knowledgeable in the ways of the spiritual life, we will see a continuation of activities such as Bible study, theology courses, prayer groups, parochial programs of all kinds, and retreats. What is often discovered in these settings is that the lay community has indeed always had a distinctive spirituality, that the graces of *heroic* love and virtue are manifest in the lay community, and that God offers the invitation to the heights of a loving relationship to *all*. The problem has been our failure to see it.

A fourth reason for a "Yes" answer—and underlying each of the others—is the essential historical character of Christianity. The God of the Hebrew scriptures and of the New Testament is a God who chooses history as the forum for self-revelation. If we are to be on the lookout for the word of God in the world, we need to pay attention to the specifics of the historical milieu. One hears the oft-repeated adage that a Christian should have the Bible in one hand and the *The New York Times* in the other. The world is the forum for God's action. In his theology, Edward Schillebeeckx reminds us of the God who takes on flesh and blood in the person of Jesus, and who desires to save us in our totality, through the very historical, existential reality of our lives. It follows that our concrete, human experiences are an essential ingredient in our understanding of the spiritual life.[8]

If this be so, then the specifics of one's lifestyle and therefore of one's daily experience are critical elements in the way we understand spirituality. This view does not deny that the gospel is one, but it does maintain that this oneness is lived out in quite different concrete circumstances in quite different ways. The moment that the gospel is lived by more than one person, it takes on a plurality of dimensions. Even the four written gospels offer quite different renditions of the one Jesus by four different communities. Further, it does not seem legitimate to reduce spirituality to "external practices," such as "particular spiritual works, pious practices, or good deeds" in order to reject the legitimate pluralism of an incarnational community and opt for what could be "cheap unity."[9]

The many volumes on priestly and religious spirituality witness to the importance of the incarnational principle.[10] Yes, we are all called to be servants, but the meaning of that service, and the condition for its possibility, lie embedded in its concrete, daily expression. Further, I suggest that such studies appear more frequently in times of duress, when the identity and/or health of such groups become endangered. I have argued that our history has left the laity without an accurate or adequate spiritual identity. Surely, given that history, we can say that the laity became an endangered species as far as the fullness of the spiritual life was considered and that they now deserve a good, corrective dose of special attention.

We see then, that lifestyle—the concrete circumstances of life—becomes an important consideration in the spiritual life. The God I discover, the images that I use, and the language I choose to describe the experience, are dependent on the specific circumstances of my life. It becomes quite significant whether I am single, married, celibate; whether I have children; whether I live alone or in community. The Christian "story" is differently appropriated by various individuals and groups and it can only be to the church's advantage to identify and include all of them in her understanding of the spiritual life.

III. THE SPIRIT BLOWS WHERE IT WILL: FREEDOM AND RESPONSIBILITY

As Christians, we need to disabuse ourselves of the fallacy that there is only *one* way to live a life of virtue. Even a cursory look at the tradition reveals a plurality of positions on virtually any issue. New experience requires continual reexamination of the meanings we assign to the spiritual life. It is important to know that the church has survived and even prospered in the midst of differing practices and doctrinal emphases. Of course, at the most general level, one can easily see the unbroken threads in the tradition, e.g., the gospel always calls Christians to imitate God in Christ and love our neighbor in the power of the Spirit. But as soon as one gets concrete and specific—what does this mean for Mary Smith in New York City in 1995?—one is launched into the process of questioning, reflecting, and discerning the complex and challenging realities of daily existence in terms of ultimate reality.

Meaning, therefore, is the product of individuals in community, using their powers of intelligence and freedom and love. It does not come from some unnameable (or nameable) place "out there" that is divorced from the workings of our own interiority. Through awareness of how we arrive at meaning and by participating consciously in this process, we take on the responsibilities of mature Christians and experience a taste of the freedom of the children of God.

We know that our freedom is not unconditional and that we are influenced at both conscious and unconscious levels by sin and personal and social forces. But these determinisms, while powerful, are not absolute. They are mitigated by one's faith in, and commitment to, the real freedom to determine meaning and to act in love. We refuse to believe that a "bad tape" inherited from parents condemns us irrevocably to a life of psychosis. Meanings that we have inherited from the past can be negotiated and *must* be negotiated if we are to be true to our best selves. Christians combat cynicism and determinism by choosing to follow Christ with love and conviction, and by opting continually to remain open to grace and to the call to live as God's friends.

It is important to emphasize the complexity of this process. There is nothing easy or automatic about getting free from centuries of non-reflective acquiescence. We have seen that as church we have a rather poor track record in this regard. But the ferment in the church since Vatican II indicates a desire and a willingness on the part of the laity to struggle with a new way of being church—one that is comparable to the kind of maturity we experience in other arenas of life.

Since the context for our discussion of spirituality is one of faith, we can say with confidence that the process of discovering the meaning structures in our lives is supported and suffused by the presence of the Spirit. A central part of the "big picture" for a person of faith is the belief that the promise of the Spirit is reliable, that grace is everywhere guiding, prompting, leading us to the truth of ourselves and of God. We are not alone, for we trust that the Spirit's power is available and being offered to us daily. Integral to the journey is growing awareness, understanding and receptivity to this life-giving breath of God.

Living consciously in the Spirit involves a readiness to allow the events of one's ordinary life, the message of the gospel, or the text of a spiritual classic to transform one's life. Since ultimately, conversion or transformation are gifts that cannot be "made" to happen, one can simply desire the gift, ask for it, and be open and ready to receive it. The Spirit functions in surprising ways. We experience the presence of the Spirit through other persons, in ecstatic moments, in times of quiet joy, in crisis and suffering, through the words of the gospel, or the text of a spiritual classic.

One does not want to be glib or naive about this readiness for God's presence. Only the foolish are unaware of the searing touch of the fire of God's love. The changes demanded along the road of holiness are not always pleasant or comfortable. And those who at some level sense the demands of the Christian life often go to great lengths to keep it at a distance. Openness to transformation requires courage, deliberation and counsel before choosing to undertake the journey.

Francis de Sales cautions against preoccupation with how we are doing in the spiritual life and always comparing ourselves to others. He would rather that Christians attend to doing their best and trust God's care to see them through. But one can ask simple, direct honest questions. Does this experience make sense to me, or am I just going through the motions? Am I blindly accepting someone else's interpretation? Is what I am doing truly contributing to making this world a better place to live?

For all the moving and high-flown ideas connected with the spiritual life, there is something down-to-earth and practical about it. God often meets us in a kind gesture in hard times, in a child's joy, a word of wisdom from a Catherine of Siena or a Julian of Norwich, a peaceful death—these are the simple but profound moments that reveal the truth and authenticity of one's life with God. It is here that things come together as we experience the total fabric of our lives and discover that it is indeed "of a piece."

NOTES

1. Bernard Lonergan, *Method in Theology* (New York: Seabury Press, 1979), pp. 57–99. 1st ed. 1972.

2. Ibid., p. 70.

3. Karl Rahner, *Foundations of Christian Faith: An Introduction to the Idea of Christianity* (New York: Seabury Press, 1978).

4. See Karl Rahner, *Theological Investigations* 7, trans. David Bourke (New York: Herder and Herder, 1971), p. 15. See also Harvey Egan, "The Devout Christian of the Future Will...be a 'Mystic': Mysticism and Karl Rahner's Theology." In *Theology and Discovery: Essays in Honor of Karl Rahner, SJ*, ed. William J. Kelly, SJ (Milwaukee, WI: Marquette University Press, 1980), pp. 139–168.

5. One of the more successful attempts at this is Dolores

Lecky's book, *The Ordinary Way* (New York, 1982), in which she adapts elements from the Benedictine rule to family life.

6. For an analysis that emphasizes the dangers of empire-building in American culture and Catholicism, see W.D. Lindsey, "The American Catholic Church and the Southern Experience: Is Integration Possible?" *New Theology Review* 5(August 1992): 45–77.

7. Richard Kieckhefer, *Unquiet Souls: Fourteenth Century Saints and Their Religious Milieu.* (Chicago: University of Chicago Press, 1984), p. 195.

8. See Edward Schillebeeckx, *Christ: the Experience of Jesus as Lord,* trans. John Bowden (New York: Seabury, 1980).

9. One example can be found in *The Ministry in the Church* by Paul Bernier (Mystic, CT: Twenty-Third Publications, 1992), p. 263.

10. Examples include Sandra Schneiders, *New Wineskins: Re-imagining Religious Life Today* (New York: Paulist Press, 1986); Mary Jo Leddy, *Reweaving Religious Life* (Mystic, CT: Twenty-Third Publications, 1990); Karl Rahner, *The Priesthood* (New York: Herder and Herder, 1973); Donald Goergen, *The Sexual Celibate* (New York: Seabury, 1974).

3

The Living Faith of the Dead: Tradition[1]

We have been attending to new developments since Vatican II and have heard the challenging call to the laity that will lead us into a new future. Now it is time to ask about the past, about those persons and traditions on whose shoulders we stand. We presuppose that history is important and that knowing and using it enhances spiritual life today. A contrary position considers history obsolete and better forgotten, but when we do not understand and use the past critically, we risk being ruled unknowingly by its dictates, as well as being deprived of its glories.

One of theology's primary tasks is to correlate the past with the present, for it is out of this correlation that the future emerges. Correlation suggests mutuality. Our present experience influences the questions we ask of the past and the ways in which we interpret that past. The tradition provides a context for the present and profoundly affects the ways we think and act in the present. The spiritual tradition refers to the classic texts, lifestyles, conscious understandings and unconscious habits that inform the spiritual life. How can the tradition legitimately influence the practice of faith—the ways in which faith becomes enfleshed in everyday actions and attitudes?

I organize my remarks under three headings: the importance of the past; problems emerging from tradition; possibilities for maximizing the rich potential of this tradition for our time.

I. THE IMPORTANCE OF THE PAST

Looking to the past is a perennial activity of the human community. Just as the many specific elements of our family environment and upbringing deeply influence who we are today, so too, on the larger canvas of history we are products of our broader past. This is certainly true in the area of spirituality, for the very way we perceive spiritual reality is heavily dependent on the persons and ideas that have preceded us.[2] The history of Western civilization shows a pattern of ways in which the community revered the past.

In the ancient Greek world, the value of an idea was contingent upon its age. Old was good and new was questionable at best. After all, a major stumbling block for the Greeks in accepting Jesus as the important figure the Christians said he was, was that he had died only a few years before. This reverence for age was exploited by persons who wanted others to pay attention to what they had written. Since present ideas about plagiarism did not exist, it was common practice to sign someone else's name (the more well-known and respected the better!), or to alter manuscripts (only to improve them, of course!) as you copied them. If you signed the name of a revered "authority," your work had a chance to be influential. A man thought to be a late fifth century Persian monk, Pseudo-Dionysius, pretended to be Dionysius, the convert of Paul, for these very reasons. Indeed, partly because of this, his *Mystical Theology* has had an immense influence on Western spirituality and mysticism, second only perhaps to the Bible and Augustine.

In the Middle Ages, society and church continued to value the past. The term "authorities" was used to designate those past illustrious writers upon whom one depended to articulate the meaning of the spiritual life. Even though a person like Thomas Aquinas (1224–1274) took liberties in altering the thought of the masters to harmonize it with his own thinking, he would have protested that he was simply echoing the authorities in a spirit of respect and reverence. Even when the meaning he assigned to a text differed significantly from that probably intended by the author, surely he felt he was being faithful to the spirit of giants like Aristotle, Augustine, and Pseudo-Dionysius. A result of this hallowing of the past meant that writers like Bonaventure (1217-1274) and Thomas Aquinas— contemporaries who lived in the same city, were appointed to chairs at the University of Paris in the same year, were probably present at each other's disputations and sermons, and even died in the same year—never even mention one another's work! A living person was incapable of being an "authority."

The Renaissance offers another example of the turn to the past, seen as a "Golden Age." In the fourteenth and fifteenth centuries, especially in Italy, we see the growing interest in and recovery of ancient Latin and Greek literature. The classical tradition became a centerpiece of the education system and a mark of culture and refinement.

Of the many possible reasons for looking to the past, I will mention two. The first is the quest for identity. We see this reflected in our own age in the recent obsession with "roots." Besides the famous television series, which can serve as a symbol for this process, we have witnessed a renewed interest in family trees; in adoptive children going to great lengths and even bringing lawsuits to discover their birth parents; in religious orders struggling to recapture the spirit of their founders; in a church that is busy examining its foundations in the scriptures and in the early Christian communities; and in the search of women and minority groups to recover histories that include their presence and accomplishments.

A second reason for a return to the past is disenchantment with the way things are in the present. When we feel discontent about some aspect of life, and begin thrashing about for ways to remedy the situation, the past often emerges as an appealing source of help—at least in groups that value tradition. One needs to beware of idealizing the past simply because it is past, or of imagining a Golden Age, which of course never existed. But when we begin to feel that we have lost our way, we turn quite naturally and legitimately to the places from which we have come to see if we can find it again. The spiritual life is no exception, and although the way is fraught with difficulties, the rewards are not insignificant.

How To Recover the Tradition

Now that we have looked at why we return to the past, we need to ask: How do we do it? I suggest that the process of critical recovery of the past involves two moments: (1) We have to try to understand the past on its own terms; (2) We have to correlate what we find there with the present. This task includes both a critique of the past and the inclusion of selected elements from the past in a new creative synthesis. Both moments offer distinct challenges and are often performed by different persons on different levels of inquiry, but they are intimately connected.

For the most part, we will have in mind what are often called "classic" spiritual texts. Examples include Augustine's *Confessions*; Bernard of Clairvaux's *Sermons on the Song of Songs;* Julian of Norwich's *Shewings;* and Teresa of Avila's *Interior Castle.* A classic can be described as a text that possesses an excess of meaning, i.e., a text that is read and reread with profit from generation to generation.[3] In the religious sphere, the Bible is the paradigmatic classic. In the secular sphere, one might mention the plays of Shakespeare or the poetry of Yeats.

In the not so distant past, the classic texts of spirituality were the best-kept secret in the church. The texts were read only by a small group of persons, usually clerics and vowed religious, and it probably never occurred to the lay community that these texts might be personally beneficial. There has also been the problem of availability of texts in reliable translations, a situation that has now changed dramatically. As the laity become more and more religiously awakened, they experience a hunger for God and a curiosity about others who have seriously pursued a spiritual journey. We are in search of language, metaphors, insight and direction from those who have gone before us. And now more than ever before, literally hundreds of texts are readily available.[4]

Understanding the past on its own terms involves the discipline of letting the figures of the past speak to us from their own times and their own structures of meaning—both sometimes very foreign to us. We must realize that there is much that we will not be able to understand. The presumption must always be that what I don't understand will probably exceed what I do. Still, it is crucial to know something about the social, political, economic, cultural milieu from which the author speaks. It is also helpful if there is some biographical data available about the person's life experience—what seemed important, traumatic, exhilarating. How did this person use language? How did she or he understand the meaning of certain terms? Against what forces were these individuals reacting in their writings or way of life?

This task requires the skills of attention, a certain level of freedom and disinterest, patience, and a good dose of historical imagination. It is very hard to understand a worldview that is significantly different from our own. The temptation is to project present meaning and understanding onto the past. But when we don't grasp the past on its own terms, we tend to absorb past ideas into the present in a literal way that creates many difficulties.

Some examples: If we look at Augustine's (354–430) statements on grace *outside* the context of the Pelagian tendencies he was opposing, they seem extreme and puzzling. Because Pelagius seemed to attribute so much power to the individual, Augustine went to the other extreme to preserve God's role as sole actor in the drama of grace. A second example involves the difficulty of understanding the preoccupation with the afterlife in the fourteenth century unless one knows of the extreme conditions of war, plague, famine and social disintegration during this period. Where does one turn when this life becomes extremely precarious and dangerous? Often spiritualities differ markedly from country to country even in the same century. For instance, one thinks of the influences on spirituality of cold, dark, northern climes and warm, balmy, southern ones.

Teresa of Avila (1515–1582) provides another example of the way understandings of the spiritual life differ from one era to another. In her writings, Teresa speaks very disparagingly about herself as a person and especially as a woman.[5] This language is quite repugnant to modern sensibilities. But if we impose our present cultural self-images, our psychological viewpoints, and our feminist consciousness on Teresa, we will fail to understand her and make the mistake of rejecting her as unenlightened. We need to know that the concept of "self-esteem," as we know it, simply did not exist in the Middle Ages and that men as well as women often referred to themselves in very humble terms when they wrote. In a similar vein, we could reject both Jesus and Paul for not speaking out against slavery or Thomas Aquinas for being a misogynist!

When we read the classics, then, we must know that it is quite different from dialogue with contemporaries. It is important to understand a spirituality on its own terms and in its own time in order to use it in our own spiritual journeys. If we recall for a moment the challenge of understanding the complexities of a person with whom we live every day, we begin to realize how difficult it is to understand someone who lived five or six or fifteen hundred years ago.

Utilizing the fruits of this first task—understanding a text on its own terms—we proceed to the task of correlating the past with our present circumstances. This task is pragmatic in nature. We test the current applicability of particular lessons from the past. Does this specific past have meaning for us today? Are there things that can help us solve problems, develop habits, or correct aberrations? Are there attitudes from the past that should be left behind, avoided at all costs? The point is not to *blame* our ancestors in the faith for not seeing what we see now, but to acknowledge that changes have occurred. One would not want to retrieve a spirituality of slavery from a time when that was an unexamined dimension of the status quo.

In this second task, we engage in discernment and decision. As we have seen, it is quite easy to agree upon ways to talk about the spiritual life in the most general and abstract of terms. Who in any age would quibble about saying that the goal of the spiritual life was union with God? Or that love was important to the journey? Or that the spiritual way involved moving from selfishness to self-transcendence? But the moment we ask what it means for a particular group or person to be united to God, or *how, specifically* one moves toward self-transcendence, we run into the specific differences of history—not to mention those of race or sex or age or geography or economic status.

I address here ways in which the past might enhance our spirituality as active, lay, late twentieth-century people. We need to ask: How can we appropriate aspects of the spiritual tradition of the Christian West?[6] Are there elements that should be left behind? What aspects of things past lend themselves to transformation in the present? What are some of the glories waiting to be rediscoverd and embraced? And what are some of the new things waiting to be born?

II. PROBLEMS OF THE TRADITION

Dualism

We note two dimensions of past spiritualities that are better left behind. The first is probably very familiar—it has been discussed over and over again in the last several decades. One danger of so much analysis is that it leads us to think that this concept is behind us, and I don't think it is. The dualistic mentality that includes a positive valuation of spirit, heaven, soul and maleness, while devaluing in significant ways, body, earth, nature, flesh, and femaleness is an entrenched attitude that dies hard. While the Christian tradition has often gone on record as one that values the struggles of this world, there is also a pervasive strain of other-worldy and anti-worldly preoccupation. Much contemporary writing on spirituality documents specific examples.[7] When we talk about a spirituality of the laity—persons whose lives are immersed in the "world" of jobs and family, bodiliness and economics—we need to remember that most classic texts were written by persons whose vocation was monastic. These authors were experts at exploring the subtle inner workings of the human spirit, but they lacked those spiritual credentials that come with facing the stresses of the marketplace, raising children and living in a committed relationship with another person until death. We need to situate texts in their historical setting and inquire about the personalities they reveal.

We need also to get beyond a too literal interpretation of the words to discover, as best we can, the meaning behind those words. Many authors use language suggesting that if one wants to advance in the spiritual life, it is good to avoid the things of the earth. In fact, in many cases, what they *mean* is that it is good not to be *attached* to the things of the earth, that is, anything but God. They counsel readers not to *cling* to things or persons, not to be so preoccupied that our ability to love freely is diminished. In some instances, a writer will go to great extremes to disparage the things of this world. When this language is transferred literally into another age—and this has too often been the case—enormous mischief is done. What is not understood is that often what the authors are disparaging is sin or anything that seems to them to be moving them away from the goal of loving union with God.

Consider, for instance, the role of the writer's personality in the ways in which she or he perceives the spiritual life. Persons who underline caution about attachment to the material world are often persons who experience in themselves an extreme passion for those very realities. Two examples from both ends of the historical spectrum are Augustine of Hippo and Dorothy Day.[8] As one reads their texts and comes closer to the persons behind them, one senses that both possessed a love for the things of this world that was so intense and so pervasive that it threatened to overrun them. Life and nature and intellect and friendship were so attractive, they felt that these could become idols and replace God in their lives. Because they knew this about themselves, they had to figure out a way to keep these things in perspective. They spoke harshly about them to order their love for the world as they thought it needed to be ordered—in harmony with the gospel as they heard it.

There is an important principle here. Our God is a God of history and works not only within the context of a given historical period, but also within the context of a given personality. Augustine and Dorothy Day may be pointing to a danger in the spiritual life that is present in some ways in every age, but it is not helpful to make these positions absolute or to regard them in abstraction from the concrete personality expressing them. It would be a spiritual catastrophe for someone who had little tendency to make idols of friendship or theater, to follow the specific ways of an Augustine or of a Dorothy Day. What is important is to identify what I do make into an idol and to take the necessary precautions.

In placing this kind of "dualism" in its proper context, I do not want to deny that there *does* exist a bias against matter in the Christian tradition. Augustine may appear to be a hero of the flesh in contrast to his Manichaean friends,[9] but the framework behind his thought, and that of the Western Christian tradition in general, is the Greek worldview in which the way to the fullness of life means escaping from the prison of the body. This backdrop operates consciously and unconsciously in the ways in which we understand spirituality and in the ways we live it in our daily lives. This bias against matter has been a serious obstacle to the full development of a lay, incarnational spirituality.

Elitism

A second problem in our tradition is the limited range of persons held up as models of holiness and the limited number of persons making the decisions about the meaning of holiness for the rest of the community. As we saw in chapter 2, our perception of holiness has been elitist in many ways. Karl Rahner is instructive on this point.[10] He spoke of the emerging " world church." After Christianity's first, predominantly Israelite stage, lasting about fifty years from the time of Jesus' death, Rahner points to a second stage, described as Western and European—that has lasted until Vatican II. He applauds a third stage, still in its infancy, in which the church recognizes its limited past and begins to open the doors to the silent ones—black, oriental, African, Hispanic, female, lay and gay voices.

We now recognize that the second stage of the spiritual tradition was dominated by monasticism and that this viewpoint has the limitations any single viewpoint inevitably has. As we open the way for others to participate in the naming of spiritual values, we can place our monastic roots in a truer perspective and enhance our appreciation of all groups in the church. Our understanding of holiness will flourish only when we begin to include all the ways in which God touches different people in their plurality and distinctiveness.

III. POSSIBILITIES OF THE TRADITION

Now that we have named some elements of the tradition that are better left behind, we should inquire how the past can enrich our spiritual quest as we move into the twenty-first century. We single out three areas: (1) elements from the past that can be helpful when transformed into a new key; (2) past glories that we need to recover and incorporate into our spiritual lives; (3) some elements that lead us into new, uncharted seas.

The Past Transformed

Two elements of the spiritual life, central in every age, are self-knowledge and community. I believe that a renewed understanding of these two realities can benefit us today in significant ways. Almost without exception, self-knowledge appears in the tradition as what I call the "first base" of the spiritual life. The meaning of self-knowledge is nuanced from writer to writer, but it has to do with at least two basic realities. First, we are creatures and sinners and second, we are made in the image and likeness of God. For most pilgrims on the spiritual journey, these are simply truths—no more and no less—that need to be in place before it makes sense to proceed on the journey. For some, this knowledge functions to get the picture in focus. We are not creators of our own existence, but owe our existence to a loving God. A natural consequence of this awareness is an attitude of thanksgiving and praise. We are sinners and therefore we need God. Likewise, we are made in God's image and likeness and are destined to return to the fullness of that reality.

In the *Interior Castle,* Teresa of Avila laments our ignorance of our true ancestry in God. She says, "It is a shame and unfortunate that through our own fault we don't understand ourselves or know who we are... We seldom consider the precious things that can be found in this soul, or who dwells within it, or its high value. Consequently, little effort is made to preserve its beauty."[11] And Catherine of Siena (1347–1380) underlines our connection with God when she repeatedly connects knowledge of self with knowledge of God. For Catherine, self-knowledge is related to the virtue of humility. She has God speak: "Here is the way, if you would come to perfect knowledge and enjoyment of me, eternal Life: Never leave the knowledge of yourself. Then, put down as you are in the valley of humility you will know me in yourself, and from this knowledge you will draw all that you need." And again, "You cannot arrive at virtue except through knowing yourself and knowing me."[12]

Upon this solid foundation from the past, we in the twentieth century have the added benefit of the growing corpus of psychological knowledge. Our sense of ourselves is quite different from that of the Middle Ages. We know more about the connections between psyche and body. We use different metaphors for human wholeness and health. The unconscious has become an integral part of the human equation. We need not belabor the point that psychology is not a replacement for spirituality, and perhaps we need to be wary at times of its encroachment beyond what it can explain, but these are not reasons to fear or dismiss it. The language and tools of psychology and human development can be of immense help to us as we journey toward union with God. The profound insights into the human psyche of our ancestors in the faith can be transformed into a new key that can provide enormous assistance to us today.

A second element is community. From one perspective it can be said that the spirituality we have inherited is markedly individualistic. But here again, some historical caveats are in order. In some cases, community existence was so taken for granted that it was rarely mentioned. And then language about the individual spiritual journey was often taken over into later historical contexts in which community existence had changed in significant ways. But in most cases, spiritual treatises were written for others—often for beginners who were asking for help in the spiritual life. Saints were encouraged to share their experience so that others in the community might be helped. But too often we view the monk in the desert or the anchoress in her hermitage falsely, as cut off from the communal context that was so central to their lives.

Today, we desire to understand and live out our spiritual lives in the context of many kinds of community. The communal aspect of our existence has been moved to center stage—not only family, professional, and ecclesial communities, but indeed, our vision now reaches out to embrace the whole cosmos. Our awareness of systemic evil has alerted us to new understandings of the milieux in which we live out the redemptive process. And we no longer look at charity as an affair between oneself and God, divorced from the demands of justice. In fact, none of the saints did either, but their efforts to help others were different in significant ways. Global awareness and social analysis have become key to our spirituality today.

Past Glories Rediscovered

The more time one spends with the classics of spirituality, the more one appreciates the depth and breadth of their content. Of the many pearls of wisdom found there, I would like to single out four. The first is the awareness in so many spiritual writers of the human potential for God. Teresa of Avila says:

> I began to think of the soul as if it were a castle made of a single diamond or of very clear crystal, in which there are many rooms, just as in heaven there are many mansions... the soul of the righteous person is nothing but a paradise, in which, as God tells us, He takes delight...I can find nothing with which to compare the great beauty of a soul and its great capacity.[13]

Because we are made in the image and likeness of God, there is no way for us to comprehend the depths of the soul. Teresa says we can hardly form any conception of the soul's great dignity and beauty. The saints seem to be in a state of constant awe at the ways God works in their lives. They are able to tell us that we can't even imagine the wonders God can bring about in our existence, challenging us to open ourselves further to grace.

Related to this potential for God is the saints' awareness of the nearness of God. One gets the sense that there is no greater obstacle to the spiritual life than thinking that God is far away. This tendency can manifest itself in a false sense of unworthiness, or in the attitude that the height of holiness is for someone else. As a result, I may become the last person in the world for whom I desire sainthood. In part, this reluctance may come from fear about the hardships that will inevitably be encountered along the way. What kind of life would I have to live if I accepted the unconditional love of God? The safety of self-protection and the familiar ruts of sin would have to be abandoned forever! Meister Eckhart (1260–1327) speaks about persons who feel that they are not up to the heroic deeds of the saints:

> ...when people find themselves unequal to this, they think that they are far away from God, and that they cannot follow God. No one ought to think this. No one ought ever under any circumstances to think himself far away from God, not because of his sins or weakness or anything else. For one does himself great harm in considering that God is far away from him; wherever a person may go, far or near, God never goes far off. God is always close at hand, and even if God cannot remain under your roof, still God goes no further away than outside the door, where he stands.[14]

Francis de Sales (1567-1622) stands out as one who was firmly convinced that people in every walk of life are called to holiness, and his life's effort, truly innovative in his day, was to help people find God in their particular life calling. The nearness of God was not the exclusive domain of any one group in the church. "True devotion," he says, "adorns and beautifies any vocation or employment."[15] He constantly opposed the tendency, frequently found among those who want to live a spiritual life, to seek the virtues of another state in life while neglecting those proper to one's own vocation.[16] The home is not a convent and the virtues of the monastic life are not lived in the same way in family life. This idea is reflected in the following statements:

> Know that God wishes nothing else of you save what he sends at the moment and do not be on the look-out for other things...What is the use of building castles in Spain when you have to live in France?[17]

> You should arrange the length of your prayer according to the number of things you have to do; and since it has pleased Our Lord to give you the sort of life which involves constant distractions, you must get used to making your

prayers short, but also so habitual that you will never omit them except for some great necessity.[18]

And again,

We are sometimes so occupied with being good angels that we neglect to be good men and women...Let us go by the land since the sea makes our head giddy...that is, the virtues which are better practised in going down than in going up....patience, putting up with our neighbor, submission, humility, meekness of heart, affability, bearing with our own imperfections...[19]

Third, the classical writers have an extraordinary grasp of the human condition. They have paid close attention to the human psyche and know its geography well. Alongside the human capacity for God run the wily and subtle tendencies toward self-deception, pride, and evasion. These "holy ones" know these deceptions well because they have struggled with them and are able to warn others against some of their pitfalls. Teresa of Avila warns her sisters against zeal that can turn into nit-picking at the minor faults of others.[20] Francis de Sales cautions against fretting over our own imperfections. He faults persons who get angry and then become angry at being angry, or disturbed at being disturbed or vexed at being vexed.[21] I have found myself repeatedly smiling at how well these holy men and women know and speak about the petty tricks and rationalizations that I know I indulge in to escape the rigors of the spiritual life. For all their eccentricities—and they are many—most saints are paragons of common sense in the world of virtue and vice.

A fourth retrievable value is the ability of so many of these masters and mistresses of the spiritual life to trust their experience of God. We may talk often and blithely of trusting our experience, but actually doing so is usually another story. Lay persons, especially, may be prone to act out of unconscious attitudes and structures of meaning inherited from the past—attitudes and meanings that may not be adequate or may not accurately reflect one's true experience. Lay persons may eschew the universal call to holiness, hiding behind the mask of pseudo-humility. In many ways, the laity have interiorized the long-standing attitude of the church that has made the heights of the spiritual life of lay persons invisible. Because the church has rarely acknowledged, affirmed or consulted the laity about the spiritual life, many lay persons are convinced that they must not have one. In such circumstances, it can be very difficult to trust, name and act on the presence of God in one's life.

After the decision is made to get on the road of the spiritual life, or after one becomes conscious that she or he has been on the road all along, the challenge of trusting what God is doing in one's life becomes central. The courage to open oneself to grace and to trust that God will work great things in us is a hallmark of the spiritual life. We are blessed with scores of role models here—from Origen (185–254), Augustine (354–430), Pseudo-Dionysius (c.500), Bernard of Clairvaux (1090–1153), Catherine of Siena (1347–1380), Julian of Norwich (c.1343–c.1416), Teresa of Avila (1513–1582), the Quaker, John Woolman (1720–1772), and Dorothy Day and Dag Hamarskjold from our own century—the list goes on and on.

In sum, I call attention to the potential of the lives and writings of our forebears to move and inspire us in our daily lives. With a bit of know-how, attention, and desire for God's love, we can experience the record of the past as a powerful motivating factor in our own spiritual journeys. No individual will be moved by every text, and a text that leaves me cold in my twenties may leave me weeping or on fire in my fifties. Personalities and styles from the past need to be matched with those in the present. But as long as the classics continue to touch us and to mediate to us the invitation to change our hearts of stone to hearts of flesh, they will survive into the future as they have survived in the past.[22]

New Horizons

We close this chapter with a few observations about the new frontiers in spirituality today—frontiers that are built upon the past, but in significant ways counteract or move beyond it.

The first frontier involves the broadening of our understanding of the ground and goal of the spiritual life—the experience of unity and community. As will be seen in more detail in chapter 4, the context for union with God today is cosmic, and the "big story" or myth of the day is the story of a continuously evolving cosmic reality. The unity in community which we seek must include not only other persons, but also embrace all forms of animate and inanimate reality.

With others, I fear that the Christian idea of the dominion of the human person over nature has led to abuses that threaten life on our planet. The daily extinction of species and rain forests and the deterioration of air and water point to problems that must be addressed in our various spiritualities.[23] As human beings, we are beginning to see ourselves as *one* image of God among many, rather than as *the* image of God to the detriment of the rest of creation. Chinese and North and South American Indian religions[24] can serve as great resources, among others, in this regard. Within this cosmic worldview, I also see a new experience of union reflected in the growing congruence between the awareness of physicists and nature mysticism. The scientist and the mystic seem to be moving ever closer to a common vision of a unified world.[25]

While not numerous, there are precedents to the broad involvement of lay persons in the spiritual life of their times. The early church welcomed a wide variety of charisms in the community as they struggled to establish themselves as church, to adapt to new movements and to defend themselves against detractors. The moving account of her imprisonment by the heroic Perpetua is replete with the images and metaphors of a new young mother struggling between the demands of an infant at the breast and those of her newly embraced Christianity. In the Middle Ages, the movement of the lay women and men called Beguines and Beghards had an often splendid, though short-lived, existence. The Reformation strove to correct the abuses of a clericalized and narrowly conceived church by elevating the status of the laity and inviting them to the fullness of gospel life. Vatican II and the experience of American Roman Catholics today form yet other chapters in this history.

What was lacking in the past and what is needed today are structures of education and support for lay persons who want to take the spiritual life seriously in all its dimensions. Past lay movements may have been short-lived in part because "ordinary" lay persons lacked the kind of personal, ecclesial or societal supports that (1) expected them to be saints, (2) provided guidance for the journey, (3) offered a community of faith which mediated and nurtured the graces of mystical union. And too often the requirements for sainthood excluded the daily round of activities that shaped the lives of all but a few in the church.

It is hard to overestimate the negative influence of these factors. Transforming them is the challenge before us. Not only must we know, criticize, and make use of the past, but we must also envision and create new worlds, new language, and new categories that will reflect the experience of the wider community—the black and yellow and female and married saints; plumber saints and teacher saints, secretary saints and mother and father saints. The vision of a spirituality that is grounded in the very fabric of daily existence points to a God who is no respector of persons, who loves without qualifications, and who remains present in the most intimate recesses of all being.

NOTES

1. See Jaroslav Pelikan, *The Vindication of the Tradition* (New Haven: Yale University Press, 1984); Gerald P. Fogarty, *"Nova et Veteris:" The Theology of Tradition in American Catholicism* (Milwaukee: Marquette University Press, 1987); George Allan, *The Importance of the Past: A Meditation on the Authority of Tradition* (Ithaca: State University of New York, 1986); Robin Maas and Gabriel O'Donnell, *Spiritual Traditions for the Contemporary Church* (Nashville: Abingdon, 1990).

2. See Alister McGrath, *A Cloud of Witnesses: Ten Great Christian Thinkers* (Grand Rapids, MI: Zondervan, 1991).

3. See David Tracy, *The Analogical Imagination* (New York: Crossroad, 1981), pp. 99–231.

4. Primary series include: *The Classics of Western Spirituality* and *Sources of American Spirituality* by Paulist Press; *Spiritual Classics and*

World Spirituality (not primary texts) by Crossroad Publishing Company.

5. *Interior Castle,* I.2.6.

6. The focus on Western Christianity is not intended to be exclusive in the sense of not recognizing the valuable contributions of other religious traditions.

7. See Matthew Fox, *Original Blessing* (Santa Fe, NM: Bear Company, 1983). Many texts today are aimed at correcting an anti-material bias, e.g., P. Campbell and E.M. McMahon, *Bio-Spirituality* (Chicago: Loyola University Press, 1985); Dody Donnelly, *Radical Love: An Approach to Sexual Spirituality* (Mpls: Winston Press, 1984); Joan Timmerman, *The Mardi Gras Syndrome: Rethinking Christian Sexuality* (New York: Crossroad, 1984); William Stringfellow, *The Politics of Spirituality* (Philadelphia: Westminster, 1984); and Dolores Lecky, *The Ordinary Way: A Family Spirituality* (New York: Crossroad, 1982).

8. *Confessions,* tr. John K. Ryan (New York: Image Books, 1960); *The Long Loneliness* (New York: Harper & Row, 1952).

9. See Margaret Miles, *Augustine on the Body* (Missoula, Montana: Scholars Press, 1979); and *Fullness of Life: Historical Foundations for a New Asceticism,* (Philadelphia: Westminster, 1981).

10. "Towards A Fundamental Theological Interpretation of Vatican II," *Theological Studies* (December, 1979): 716–727.

11. *Interior Castle,* I.1.2.

12. *The Dialogue,* (New York: Paulist Press, 1980), pp. 29, 88, 118, etc.

13. *Interior Castle,* I.1.1.

14. "Counsels on Discernment," 17. In *Meister Eckhart* (New York: Paulist Press, 1981), p. 266.

15. *Introduction to the Devout Life,* I.3. Tr. John K. Ryan, (New York: Harper & Row, 1950).

16. Jean Pierre Camus, *The Spirit of St. Francois De Sales* (New York: Harper & Row, 1952), p. 206.

17. *St. Francis De Sales in His Letters,* edited by The Sisters of the Visitation (London: Sands & Co., 1933), p. 76.

18. *Selected Letters,* tr. Elizabeth Stopp (London: Faber & Faber, 1960), p. 204.

19. *St. Francis De Sales in His Letters,* pp. 78–79.

20. *Interior Castle,* I.2.16.

21. *Introduction,* III.9.

22. There are growing numbers of studies that focus on productive ways to use the past in our present situation. Examples include:

Elizabeth A. Dreyer, *Passionate Women: Two Medieval Mystics* (New York: Paulist Press, 1989); John Welch, *Spiritual Pilgrims* (New York: Paulist Press, 1982; and Roberta C. Bondi, *To Pray and To Love* (Minneapolis: Fortress Press,1991).

23. See Thomas Berry, *The Dream of the Earth* (California: Sierra Club, 1988); John Cobb, *Is It Too Late?* (Beverly Hills, CA: Bruce, 1972) and *God and the World* (Philadelphia: Westminster, 1969); Loren Eiseley, *The Immense Journey* (New York: Time, Inc., 1962); Joseph G. Donders and Elizabeth Byrne, *Original Joy* (Mystic, CT: Twenty-Third Publications, 1989).

24. See Joseph Epes Brown, *The Spiritual Legacy of the American Indian* (New York: Crossroad, 1982); Ake Hultkrantz, *Belief and Worship in Native North America* (New York: Syracuse University Press, 1981); Elisabeth Tooker, ed., *Native North American Spirituality of the Eastern Woodlands* (New York: Paulist Press, 1979); Miguel Leon-Portilla, ed., *Native Mesoamerican Spirituality* (New York: Paulist Press, 1980).

25. See Brian Swimme, *The Universe Is a Green Dragon* (Santa Fe, NM: Bear & Co., 1983).

4

Theological Roots: Holy Spirit, Creation and Incarnation

A spirituality that takes everyone in the community into account needs to be grounded theologically. Common sense may indicate that a more inclusive spirituality of everyday life is long overdue, but this is not enough. Sooner or later, we will start to wonder about how this vision is grounded biblically and theologically. What kind of theology validates this vision?

Authentic theology is derived from the Spirit life of the faith community and, in turn, influences and shapes that life. We have begun to examine the importance of daily experience in our grasp of the spiritual life. Experience also grounds theology and in turn, theological expression gives voice to, and influences, human behavior. An authentic theology not only accurately reflects the lived experience of the community, but it informs and quickens behavior as well, motivating the community to more virtuous living and deeper self-understanding. Amidst the many theological sea changes experienced by the church in the recent past, three theological topics are especially pertinent to our topic: the Holy Spirit, creation and incarnation.

These theological emphases arise out of renewed attention to contemporary experience. Prior to Vatican II, many in the church felt a gap between their "real" lives and the theology governing church polity and practice. But then the church invited us to "read the signs of the times" and to nurture a new openness to the values of the modern world. The renewal of these aspects of theology can only assist the integration of daily existence within the horizon of ultimate meaning in which our lives are lived.

I. THE HOLY SPIRIT[1]

When I ask groups to describe what they understand by the term "spirituality," hardly anyone ever mentions the Holy Spirit. This has always struck me as odd. Initial responses to the question are panic-stricken looks and a flurry of attempts to say *something*. The answer seems obvious until one tries to pin it down. But the word itself is instructive. Spirituality must have something to do with "spirit" if not with "Holy Spirit."

Unfortunately, at least in some parts of the Christian tradition, the Holy Spirit has been the Cinderella figure, neglected and quasi-invisible.[2] As a result, theological reflection on the Spirit remains a major project. Theological language about the Holy Spirit will emerge as we continue to reflect on the ways in which we experience the Holy Spirit in our prayer and daily lives.

The Hebrew scriptures speak of the breath (*ruah*) of God (Gen 6:3: Ps 104:29), of the wind as a symbol of God's power (Ex 10:13), of the power of the prophets (Judg 6:34). The metaphors of breath and wind suggest reflection on the Spirit in terms of air and breathing and the important life-function they play. The New Testament extends this power to all God's people (Acts 2), portraying the Spirit as a power (*dynamis*) that enables us to love, to live in the fullness of new life in Christ. Theologians emphasize the experiential character of the Spirit's presence, often speaking of it as a feminine force, nurturing, enabling, empowering. Let us focus on three ways in which the Christian community speaks about the Holy Spirit.

Spirit as Gift

Perhaps more than any other name for the Spirit, "Gift" has held a preeminent place in the tradition. Theologian Yves Congar says, "the Spirit is the principle of love and realizes our lives as children of God in the form of a Gift, fulfilling that quality in us."³ We also speak of the "gifts" and "fruits" of the Holy Spirit—those virtuous qualities that reveal the presence of the Spirit within. Within the Trinity, the Spirit is seen as the expression of the mutual love of God and Christ. This expression of love that is the Holy Spirit is offered to us as a gift enabling us to grow in divine likeness and to carry on the work of redemption in time.

For the most part, we receive the gift of the Spirit mediated through human relationships. To receive this gift is to receive life. To know that we receive the Spirit as gift from others is to live a life of gratitude and praise. One of the signs of growth in the spiritual life is that one sees all of life, including its pain and sorrows, as gift of God. An unattractive alternate disposition is to experience life as "owing" us something. Inevitably life never measures up to what we think we are "owed," bringing pettiness, cynicism and despair in its wake.

The supreme aspect of the gift of the Spirit to us is a unifying love. The effect of the Spirit's presence among us is to build creation into a community. This gift can be received and acted upon in every aspect of life. From the family and neighborhood to the factory and office, our attitudes and behaviors either build up community or tear it down. The Spirit works in and through us to create harmony and unity within ourselves and in our relationships with others and with the world.

This Spirit-power takes many forms. Underlying all of them is the realization that all of life is gift. In a recent novel, *Mariette in Ecstasy*, Ron Hansen puts these words into the mouth of a contemplative sister at the turn of the century.

> Ever since I have grown older, I have forgotten all my hard penances and fasting and have given particular attention to our Redeemer, in whose presence we live. And I have realized how much simpler it is to pray and keep united with God when I see Him as the source and sum of everything I do. When I walk, I owe it to God that I still can. When I sleep, it is with His permission. My breathing, my happiness, even my being a woman—all are His gifts to me. So it is my prime intention that whenever I do these practical

things, they will be contemplative acts of praise and thanksgiving repeated over and over again.[4]

One does not need to live in a contemplative monastery to
have these sentiments. Anyone can dwell in this awareness and
look upon existence with a grateful gaze, a loving and compassionate regard that is creative of a loving unity. Thomas Merton
reminds us that gratitude is the heart of a contemplative existence. And at the heart of a life of gratitude is that Gift we call
Spirit.

Spirit as Contact Point Between God and Humans[5]

The spiritual life is about knowing and loving God. This
loving knowledge of God in Christ is made possible by the Holy
Spirit. One can think of the Spirit as God experienced in intimate communion. The presence of the Spirit of God is necessarily diffuse (hence, metaphors like breath and wind), since it
permeates all aspects of the Christian life. The Spirit has not
been personified in the same way as the other persons in the
Trinity—God/Mother/Father and Jesus Christ—thus remaining
more susceptible to endless varieties of expression. In a sense,
we are a personification of the Spirit in our distinct individuality as images of God.

In her book, *God For Us*, Catherine LaCugna speaks of the
"self-effacing" nature of the Spirit. Because the Holy Spirit is
always the means to God and never the end in itself, it is impossible to specify exactly what the Spirit is in itself. The Spirit's
role is to "lead persons to other persons, to bring creatures into
union with God."[6] One might say that the Holy Spirit is the condition of the possibility of holiness. The Spirit enables us not
only to know God but to respond to God's self-gift in love. The
Spirit is the energy enabling us to become saints.

To understand the Spirit in this way is to emphasize both
immanence and transcendence. On the one hand, because God
is so utterly mysterious and beyond us, we need the Spirit to
acknowledge in faith that this God has chosen to come among
us in the person of Jesus Christ as Lord. On the other hand, the
Spirit works within us in ways that are closer to us than we are

to ourselves. The Spirit is identified in intimate ways with the faith community. At Pentecost the Spirit was sent forth as God *among us.*

We begin to see the essential role that the Spirit plays in the spiritual life. Perhaps because the Spirit is so omnipresent, and therefore amorphous, we have difficulty speaking of it and tend to neglect it. But with renewed vision and sensitivity, we begin to notice and appreciate that the Spirit works everywhere—within us, within our communities and within our world—that this grace is everywhere connecting the human with the divine in ever-new and creative ways.

The Spirit as Creative Power

We begin with a paradox. We speak about God being all-powerful and yet as Christians, baptized into grace, we believe that we truly have a share in divine power. How *do* we talk about human spiritual power? To begin, we say that it is the work of the Spirit, not in the sense of something added on to human existence, but rather as something intrinsic to our very beings as created and loved by God. At times we have understood divine and human power in inverse relationship. This view holds that when we attribute spiritual power to humans we somehow diminish God's power. But there is another way to look at human spiritual power. If the Spirit was sent to empower us to continue the work of redemption, then the more spiritual power humans possess, the more is the power of God enhanced, not diminished.

This power is a gift and we are free to accept or reject it. Power is an energizing, enabling, animating reality. It is the ability to act, to bring something or someone into being, into life. The Spirit, the power of God in Christ, does not obliterate our power as humans, but enhances it, enabling us to effect change for the good. Paul's letter to the Ephesians seems particularly relevant in our own day:

> I pray that, according to the riches of his glory, he may grant that you may be strengthened in your inner being with power through his Spirit, and that Christ may dwell in

your hearts through faith, as you are being rooted and grounded in love. I pray that you may have the power to comprehend, with all the saints, what is the breadth and length and height and depth, and to know the love of Christ that surpasses knowledge, so that you may be filled with all the fullness of God. (Eph 3:16 - 19, NRSV).

Unfortunately, the term "power" often carries with it negative connotations and we shy away from it. This fear is well-founded in the sense that we are all too familiar with human power gone awry, power placed at the service of greed and egoism. But the threat of the misuse of power should not make us shy away from the serious responsibility we have as Christians to assent to our own participation in the power of God for the good of the world.

Such a pneumatology legitimates a spirituality of everyday life. More than in any other place, we exercise Spirit-power in our ordinary, at-times-humdrum, at-times-marvelous, lives. God's power revealed in Jesus is a healing, forgiving, uplifting, loving power. We are called, in the Spirit, to exercise this power as we go about our daily rounds. In the context of this daily arena we become saints or sinners. In the Spirit, we are empowered to follow Jesus' example, offering these gifts to others.

Creation is often what we think of first when we think of God's power. But this initial creative act extends itself in endless ways throughout the cosmos and time. The very sending of the Word into history to take on flesh and share with us all the joys and sorrows of being human is an incredible act of God's creative and imaginative power. In this context we can think about the Spirit as one who empowers us, who gives us confidence and courage to develop and use this power in a creative, healing and unifying way. In Christ's Spirit we have the power to bring about something new in ourselves in others and in the world.

II. CREATION

The Judeo-Christian story, while dependent on preceding cultures and religious experiences, begins its written history with Genesis and the story of creation. This is one aspect of our tradition that has taken on new meaning in the midst of an ecological crisis. The refrain of the creation story, repeated over and over again—"And it was good"—is a foundational truth of the spiritual life. A good God is the Creator of good things. Our world, the earth, and all that is in it, is good. The story goes on to relate that something went wrong with this picture, marring the inherent goodness in the world. But the advent of sin does not change the *starting point* of the story, i.e., the creation of a good world by a good and loving God.

One also chooses a starting point for one's theology or spirituality, and the substance and orientation of a spirituality depend on this choice. Some theologians criticize the past for focusing too exclusively on sin as the starting point. They are not suggesting that we eliminate sin from the theological picture, but rather that we place our awareness and experience of sin in the more primordial experience of a good creation.

A second foundational aspect of the Genesis story is the account of our creation in the image and likeness of God. What would our spiritualities be like if we took this part of the story with utmost seriouness? God, the awesome, loving Mystery creates us in this very image. The image has been distorted by sin, but the presence of sin does not negate the original intention of God, nor the original goodness of creation. In fact, greater appreciation of the goodness of creation can only lead to a deeper sense of the horror and seriousness of sin.

Culture

When we place creation truly at the center of our picture we embrace all of culture—the artifacts created by human beings throughout time. William Stringfellow uses the term "politics" to talk about this aspect of spirituality. For him, politics "refers to the total configuration of relationships among humans and institutions and other principalities and the rest of created life in this world."[7] This includes art and education and factories; medicine and the law; churches and families.

In the past, we erred on the side of separating creation

and culture. This separation resulted too often in a romanticized version of nature and a demonized version of culture. As we will see in chapter 5, churches can be accused of despising and denigrating culture, seeing it as an evil force rather than as a human extension of God's creative activity. Cultures can and do become seriously co-opted by sin, but our theology has always held that this flaw, however destructive, is not fatal and cannot obliterate the goodness of God's presence.

A major sign of the recovery of our understanding of the goodness of culture is the attention and respect with which we regard the diversities in our midst. The global village has made us aware as never before of the multifarious ways in which persons live, govern and believe. On the one hand, our differences tear us apart with bias, hatred, war and revenge. On the other hand, we struggle mightily to accept and value the multicultural environment in which we live—the wealth of difference in language, and the ways that family events, birth and death are celebrated. Many U.S. churches work hard to be inclusive of diverse cultures, manifesting for our own time Thomas Aquinas' insight that the more diverse the world, the more praise and glory we are able to render to God.[8]

If politics, in the sense of the total configuration of relationships among humans and institutions, describes the work of the Word in the world, then spirituality "represents the *ordinary* experience of discerning and partaking in these politics. It is that very estate into which people are baptized. It is the same circumstance which, in the origins of the church of Jesus Christ, entitled every baptized person to be called *saint*. So it was, long ago. In truth, so it is today."[9]

Cosmos

We are created embodied spirits. Not only are we made up of material and spiritual elements, but we are intimately connected with the larger material universe. It is unfortunate that we continue to embrace past patterns of thought which held that the way to become spiritual was to flee things material and bodily. Now it seems quite foolish, when one considers the extent to which we have equated the spiritual life, or holiness, with escaping who we were originally created to be, How can becoming holy/whole involve denying any integral aspect of our existence?

With growing scientific capabilities to discover, study, and participate in the cosmos—galaxies and solar systems—we are increasingly aware of the vast universe in which we exist. The image of the earth from space has changed decisively our conception of reality. Now appropriate changes in our self-understanding must follow. We must grapple with our anthropocentric preoccupations and confront a false anthropology that views human persons in isolation from their cosmic moorings.

Our forgetfulness of nature, with its rhythms and cycles, has some roots in the very origins of monotheism. In order for Israel to remain true to the one God, Yahweh, she had to define herself over against the gods of the surrounding cultures. Many of these religions endowed natural realities with divine status. Religious ritual was centered around the agricultural seasons of planting and harvesting. Sun, moon and stars were sacred realities, revered and connected with human life. As a result of opposing these forces, the community gradually lost sight of the sacred dimensions of natural reality, moving the Judeo-Christian religion away from nature toward an almost exclusive focus on history.

In part because of this history, we are now struggling to reconnect our understanding of the sacred with all reality. The Judeo-Christian myth,[10] with its emphasis on the human species and on history, needs to be further informed by the myth of the evolution of species.[11] In addition to seeing ourselves as image of God, we need to see ourselves as one species among many, the fruit of millions of years of molecular activity. We are now acutely aware that we have the power to destroy this tiny planet earth, either through nuclear destruction or ecological abuse, and that, in any event, the universe will go on its appointed rounds after us as it did before us.[12]

The theory of evolution affords us a valuable and true look at the ways in which we are connected with all animate and inanimate reality. It gives us a fresh, less self-centered perspective and has the potential to draw us close to matter at all levels. Awareness of the interconnectedness of all parts of reality helps us realize how very mutual and interdependent existence is. The human species has a special and awesome function in the universe. It is the species that provides the self-aware, thinking, loving dimension for the entire cosmos. Polluted water and air remind us of the ways in which other species provide us with the very means of sustenance and of the terrifying potential humans have to destroy the balance. A renewed theology of creation will reflect these concerns and function as a catalyst for future ecologically responsible behavior.

To live in hope as we face possible ecological disaster is a difficult and revolutionary activity. Such hope has got to be one of the pillars of any contemporary spirituality. The mandate of the gospel is to respond to every grace, to use every resource available to us in the service of our world.

Part of this task will be to envision a God who is really and dynamically involved in a mutual relationship with nature and culture. The notion of a God who has a logical, but not real, relation to the world is not adequate. We need to find ways to talk about God that connect God with nature and culture in real and integral ways. To denigrate nature or culture is to denigrate God. As Christians we must abandon our penchant to be abusers of nature and despisers of culture. This does not mean that we abandon the Christian responsibility to take a critical, prophetic stance against the sin of the world. But the locus of our criticism has to be *within* the community of humankind, world and universe—not over against it. We need to be vigilant against both pseudo-scientism, i.e., harmful technology fueled by greed, *and* a theology that tries to force the universe into narrow biblical categories or reduce it to constricting theological constructs.[13]

In the Christian story, history and the cosmos are not the final word. The end, the culmination, the fullness of the story takes place beyond history. But in the meantime, natural and cultural creation is the forum in which all believers receive and work out their salvation. In addition, we profess that the story-in-progress and the end of the story are not divorced from each other. The fulfillment of the final moment is already present with us in part. Christianity holds that the ongoing saga of the divine-human rapprochement has reached a highpoint in the incarnation, which permits a glimpse, a genuine foretaste of the fullness of life to come.

III. INCARNATION

The messages enfolded in the incarnation are many. Incarnation reveals a God who is courageous, whose gestures reveal an unfathomably generous love in a willingness to communicate and give God's self in the world for us. The event of incarnation has also had a profound effect on the world. It makes holy every cubic inch of reality from quarks to human beings—cosmos, world, flesh, matter, spirit. The incarnation brings new meaning to the "it was good" of the Genesis story. Material creation, embodiment, history, have been irrevocably transformed because of the union of the human and the divine. We can no longer speak glibly of the sacred and the profane as opposing realities. Therefore, our task as Christians is not to "bring" Christ to the world, but to be on the lookout, to discover and uncover the Christ that is already present. Sin and fear blind us to this reality, preventing us from seeing the truth and the incredible ramifications of this event.

Part of our task in Part II will be to see what a spirituality looks like that takes these realities seriously. In the light of our inherited tradition, how can we understand a spirituality today that is as fully cognizant of created, embodied, historical, redeemed existence as it is of the spirit and of sin? What meanings can we fashion which will maximize the realization of the goals of the spiritual life, which will assist us to become free, whole and loving individuals, moved to compassion and to action for a just world?

We aim for a much stronger and more radical sense of the meaning of incarnation in our lives. *All* of matter, *all* of the cosmos has been *radically* and *unalterably* made holy by the entrance of God into history.

Conclusion

Equipped with these theological resources—Spirit, creation and incarnation—we pursue our spiritual journeys in the ordinary and extraordinary happenings of everyday life. These journeys will be marked by dispositions and attitudes upheld by the theological emphases we have just discussed. Below is a summary of several salient points culled from this discussion.

1. I suggest that we begin to see ourselves more and more as a part of the universe. The human person is one important dimension or mode of being in a vast network of interconnected realities. We might look at ourselves as the reflexive, self-conscious mode of the cosmos, a mode whose function in the totality of creation is reflective awareness. Can we begin to see ourselves as a truly integral part of the world, as truly interdependent with trees and water, and topsoil?

This awareness is humbling. It permits a sense of love, awe, and respect for other modes of being. It creates a sacramental awareness that allows us to see and celebrate God in God's creation. Finally, it results in a new consciousness which demands ecological responsibility. Our resources here include Francis of Assisi, Chinese, and Native American spiritualities.[14]

2. We are called to see ourselves as members of the human community rather than over against it. This awareness allows us to grow in our ability to experience the joys and sufferings of others as our own—from the members of our immediate family to our friends, to those across the globe. It puts the primary focus on the second part of the great commandment—love of neighbor. In the *Interior Castle,* Teresa of Avila posits that we can never know for sure if we are loving God, so she advises her sisters to focus on love of neighbor, knowing that if one is loving one's neighbor, one can be sure one is loving God as well. The virtue of hospitality is relevant in this context. Hospitality is a virtue that seems almost inexhaustible in its applications, correcting the mistrust and inhospitality in and around us.

This sense of being an integral member of the human community challenges us to discern what is truly good for that community and to trust our ability to perform this good. From our own experience and wisdom, we do have some sense about what is good for ourselves and others, and a future spirituality will involve acting upon these insights.

3. A third point is a corollary to the second. Membership in the human community immerses us in relationships of every stripe. Often our knowledge of human relationships can be a great help in understanding and nurturing our relationship with God. Without equating the two, one can see that human relationships provide valuable information about one's relationship with God. We are basically the same person whether we are conversing with a friend or addressing God in prayer. One can reflect on (a) the awareness of the giftedness of true, loving relationships; (b) the ability to respond to or refuse that love; (c) the knowledge of why we choose to be aware of and spend time with the beloved—or not; (d) who speaks and who listens, when and how often; (e) whether we understand how love leads to commitment and what this means; (f) what our strengths and weaknesses are as partners in relationships and how these are affecting our relationships with others and God.

4. Attention to quotidian experience underlines the importance of discovering each person's unique path. While the tradition offers us many wonderful roadmaps, each of us needs to put together a "way in the Spirit" that suits our particular personality, experience, gifts and stage in life. This process may involve becoming acquainted with some of the options in the tradition, but above all it involves paying attention to the ways in which the Spirit is working in each of our lives—the nudges, the subtle movements, or perhaps the brilliant flashes—that will be missed if we are not in tune with them.

Spirituality has to do with the way we actually experience joy, suffering, integration, the truly real, the authentic. This is opposed to a way filled with pessimism, despair, dichotomies, and illusion. We need to pay attention to the ways Mystery is emerging in our lives—the ways in which we are called to genuine love of self and neighbor.

5. One can begin one's quest by attending to the desires of the heart, both personal and communal. The Spirit is revealed in our genuine hopes for ourselves and for the world. In terms of both daily life and ultimate reality, what do we truly want for ourselves? Desire is a cornerstone in almost every spiritual clas-

sic. Desire functions as the fuel that drives the whole journey and it seems to me to be a neglected aspect of the spiritual life. How much do we *want* holiness for ourselves and others? How brightly burns the flame of desire for a love affair with God, other persons and the cosmos? Do we *know* that to desire and seek God is a choice that is always available to us?

6. Finally, in spite of a world that threatens to overwhelm us with violence, anxiety and anguish, can we learn to relax and enjoy? Can we imagine ourselves in the role of Wisdom at the dawn of creation?

> Then I was at God's side each day,
> God's darling and delight,
> playing in God's presence continually,
> playing on the earth, when God had finished it,
> while my delight was in humankind (Prov 8:30–31).

Meister Eckhart and Francis de Sales counsel us to pay attention gently, to trust, not to "sweat the small stuff," not to worry about how we are doing, but to let go.

> We must not fret over our own imperfections. Although reason requires that we must be displeased and sorry whenever we commit a fault, we must refrain from bitter, gloomy, spiteful, and emotional displeasure. Many people are greatly at fault in this way. When overcome by anger, they become angry at being angry, disturbed at being disturbed, and vexed at being vexed. By such means they keep their hearts drenched and steeped in passion.[15]

And again,

> The care and diligence with which we should attend to our concerns are very different from solicitude, worry and anxiety. The angels have care for our salvation and are diligent to procure it, yet they are not solicitous, worried, and anxious. Care and diligence may be accompanied by tranquillity and peace of mind...Don't be worried about them [the matters God commits to our care], for worry disturbs reason and good judgment and prevents us from doing well the very things we are worried about.[16]

7. And finally, as Christians, we are offered Jesus, the incarnate God as model. For our needs today, I suggest that Jesus might best be seen in his simplicity. He was a man who lived a life with, for, and open to others. His life was basically an active one, immersed in the affairs of his world, with an occasional time apart when an important decision was afoot. The witness of his life continually calls us to a mature discipleship, to be followers emulating his direct simplicity and his loving, self-sacrificing spirit.

In such a Spirit-filled, creation and incarnation centered view, how would the basic tenets of the spiritual life need to be changed, e.g., our idea of sin, of the virtues, of relationships and sexuality as loci of the holy, of the development, methods and progress in the spiritual life, of the fruits of holiness, of the roles of intellect and emotion in the spiritual life? How deeply do we understand rules for discernment? What does the tradition offer that might assist us in this task, and what needs to be avoided?

A theology that gives Spirit, creation, and incarnation their due provides a solid resource for our practical engagement in the business of becoming saints. It is to the daily round of loving, working and praying that we now turn in pursuit of some answers to these questions.

NOTES

1. Perhaps the most well-known major study of the Holy Spirit is Yves Congar's three-volume, *I Believe in the Holy Spirit* (New York: The Seabury Press, 1983). French original, 1979. See also J. Patouit Burns & G.M. Fagin, *The Holy Spirit* (Wilmington, DE: Glazier, 1984), and Richard J. Hauser, *Moving in the Spirit* (New York: Paulist, 1986).

2. Pentecostal and charismatic Christian groups give a central role to the Holy Spirit. Also, the Eastern Church has always been known for the privileged place it affords the Spirit in both its theology and practice. These groups can serve as resources for us as we develop new pneumatological theologies.

3. Ibid., vol. 2, p. 67.

4. Ron Hansen, *Mariette In Ecstasy* (New York: Edward Burlingame Books, 1991), pp. 67–68.

5. See K. McDonnell, "A Trinitarian Theology of the Holy Spirit," *Theological Studies* 46 (1985):219.

6. Catherine LaCugna, *God For Us* (San Francisco: Harper, 1992), p. 362.

7. *The Politics of Spirituality,* p. 26.

8. Thomas Aquinas, *Summa theologiae* I, q. 47.

9. *The Politics of Spirituality*, p. 26.

10. By "myth" I mean the overarching story that inspires and guides the meaning structures and behaviors of a community. In this sense "myth" is the polar opposite of what is false. A "myth" is a story about realities whose truth is so profound that only a story can begin to capture it. Ordinary, everyday language is simply not adequate. Myths answer questions such as: Who is God? What is love? What is death? What is evil? How can we get along with each other? In religious terms one can point to the Buddhist, Jewish, Confucian, Islamic or Christian "myths."

11. "The scientific enterprise has produced a creation myth that offers humanity a deeper realization of our bondedness, our profound communion not only within our own species, but throughout the living and non-living universe." Brian Swimme, "Science: A Partner in Creation," in *Thomas Berry and the New Cosmology* ed. Anne Lonergan (Mystic, CT: Twenty-Third Publications, 1988), p. 86.

12. Happily there is a rapidly growing corpus of literature on this and related topics. A sampling might include: I. G. Barbour, *Western Man and Environmental Ethics* (Englewood Cliffs, NJ: Prentice Hall, 1973); John Bennett, "Nature—God's Body?" in *Philosophy Today* (Fall, 1974): 248–254; P. Joranson and K. Butigan, eds. *Cry of the Environment: Rebuilding the Christian Creation Tradition* (Santa Fe, NM: Bear & Co., 1984); Sallie McFague, *Models of God: Theology for An Ecological Nuclear Age* (Philadelphia: Fortress Press, 1987). See also chapter 3 above, notes 23–25.

13. Brian Swimme laments: "Scientists dropped out of religion because theologians and preachers had nothing interesting to say about the universe. Then, too, they stopped sitting in the pews because the preachers kept explaining to them that their passions and interests, their meaning, their central devotions in life are unimportant—or irrelevant and footnotes to the real truth." *Science, A Partner in Creation,* p. 85. Pierre Teilhard de Chardin springs to mind in this context as one who devoted his life to bringing these two worlds together, and paid a rather high price for it.

14. One is invited to reflect on the differences between the Native American baptismal custom of offering the child *to* the water,

and our Western custom of *using* the water to baptize the child. In the Middle Ages, awareness of being connected with the larger universe was symbolized in the custom of offering a newborn to the moon so that the cosmos might be favorably disposed toward the child during life.

15. Francis de Sales, *Introduction to the Devout Life,* III.9.
16. Ibid., III.10.

PART II
BUILDING BLOCKS FOR
A SPIRITUALITY OF
EVERYDAY LIFE

Introduction

The foundations laid in Part I compel us to look at ordinary, everyday experience as a sacred realm that is the primary locus for the spiritual life. In Part II, we turn to those everyday experiences that are the building blocks of the spiritual life. A creative examination of these activities, in light of a theology of Spirit, creation and incarnation, reveals that they cannot be seen as ancillary, much less as a hindrance, to holiness. On the contrary, they are the very heart of the spiritual life for all baptized Christians.

Chapters 5 through 8 examine the struggle, love and work that are at the heart of human life. These experiences, whether unremarkable or heroic, present to us the worldly face of God and are the primary means to holiness. Chapter 9 explores the meaning of self-sacrifice in this everyday context. Chapters 10 and 11 take a fresh look at the more explicitly religious activities of the individual and of the community—contemplation and liturgy.

The aim is to broaden and transform the categories in which we have traditionally understood the journey into God, making ordinary life the center of that journey. In each area, we draw attention to how an incarnational theology requires new, more inclusive ways of thinking about holiness, and to how the tradition can be used as a constructive, rather than as a limiting, resource for a spirituality of everyday life.

5

The Worldly Face of God: A Spirituality of Everyday Life

> Will you, God, really live with people on earth?
> Why, the heavens and their own heavens cannot contain
>   you.
> How much less this house that I have built...
> Day and night let your eyes watch over this house, over
>   this place of which you have said,
> "My name shall be there."
>
> (1 Kgs 8:27–29)

One does not require an advanced degree to notice that the post-Vatican II church is reeling, struggling with change and with the new, vibrant breath of the Spirit that is blowing through the community. Our attempt at renewal has caused us to reexamine the church, the sacraments, spirituality, religious life, priesthood and the laity. We are taking modern experience more seriously, which is forcing us to change the way we do theology, and the way we understand ourselves as humans, as citizens and as believers. We are renewing our connections with the joys and the plight of the world, with the result that the totality of life becomes the arena in which we experience God.

At an earlier stage, the sacred and the secular were set off from one another. God spoke within the realm of the sacred and this voice armed us against the evils of the "world." Then we began to grapple at a deeper level with the truth of an incarnated God and discovered that the strict separation of sacred and secular was no longer adequate. The discoveries of psychology gave us new insights into what it means to be human and our faith struggled to take account of this information. A faith that works against these new insights about what it means to be human is destined to atrophy and die. And if the "world" in and of itself is not evil, then we need to attend more carefully to the process of discernment. Sin and suffering are the enemy, not the "world," and sin is clearly present—not only in the "world" but also within each person and within the church.

A further step, now, involves a reversal. Not only is everyday experience no longer to be seen as an obstacle to being holy, but rather, it is to be understood as the *primary* forum for the journey toward holiness. Not only do we look at prayer as a space in which to become truly human, but we look at being truly human as the primary space for prayer.

For everyone, the spiritual life involves the connections we make between the divine and the human. But the lives of clergy, vowed religious, and professional ministers are steeped in explicit, public, religious symbols and activity. Public ordination and taking vows, celebrating liturgy, regular formal prayer, teaching religious education, doing spiritual direction, are activities that have God as their direct and proper object. However, most members of the church spend their days in a world that is not at all explicitly religious. Therefore, it becomes imperative that this wider lay community be empowered to see God on its daily rounds—wherever that may be. We need to build up our confidence in our ability to open ourselves to the grace through which we find God in all the nooks and crannies, in all the agony and stress and frustration of life, and not just in overtly religious experiences.

At times God will be known in the experience of absence. Experiences of broken relationships, stress, burnout, frustration and hopelessness are a particular challenge to faith. Too often our ability to see this world as a sacrament of divine mystery must seem extremely fragile. The complexity and ambiguity of existence can threaten to undermine our belief. But the invitation remains for each of us to persevere, and to grow in our trust in God's desire to be lovingly present to us in all circumstances of daily life.

If we truly believe that all events and moments in our lives have the capacity to mediate God's presence to the world, then each person will experience God and follow the spiritual path in her or his unique way. The primary responsibility for discovering God's presence in our lives and in our world is ours. We cannot expect clergy, professional ministers or the liturgy to do this for us. The ultimate goal of the theology and spirituality presented here is that readers will come to a deeper realization of their own desire for God; cultivate a profound love and reverence for their own concrete existence and for the world, with all its sorrows and joys; mature in their ability to find God in places that they never thought possible before; and to trust that experience as the heart of their spiritual lives. What are some examples of the ways in which we encounter the worldly face of God?

Nature

Often one's earliest awareness of God is mediated through the power and beauty of nature. The gentle curve of the shore along the ocean; the roaring sea in a storm; the sky at sunset from Maine to Montana; the majesty of snow-capped mountains; or the intricate delicacy of a budding flower or a spider's web.

Closer to home, we witness neighborhood trees budding and grass growing in the spring; a gentle summer rain; lightning and thunder seen and heard from the front porch; shoveling mounds of snow, making snowpeople and angels and having snowball fights. We mourn over a tree that needs to be felled because of disease, and we tramp through the leaves on an autumn evening. God whispers or sometimes shouts at us through these phenomena of nature.

We are free to take the time, to notice, to appreciate, to be in awe. We are free to pass this awareness on to our children, our friends, our colleagues. Poets and painters, and photographers and film makers assist us by keeping the wonderful images of nature before us. Indeed, the "world is charged with the grandeur of God."[1]

Physicists bedazzle us with theories of the origins and development of the universe. Theories of chaos and the "big bang" intrigue us, as do the intricacies of the space/time continuum and black holes. Ecologists confront us with the truth that we are a significant but small part of the universe. We are young children in a universe that is millions of years old. They press us to see the universe as a living, breathing thing, as an enormous complex of systems. Our relationship with these systems is one of interdependence and sister/brotherhood. And we weep at the slow, methodical destruction of our ecosystem. If we have the eyes to see, the natural world constantly reflects the dialectic of the presence and the absence of God.

Personal Relationships

In addition to finding God in nature, we treasure God's presence in our relationships with other human beings. The web of human connections is perhaps the preeminent place in which most people report experiences of God's self-revelation. We all belong to many human communities, but none touches us so deeply as the family.[2] The family often becomes the crucible in which we are initially formed through experiences of presence/absence of spirit. This responsibility for formation is then passed on from generation to generation, with both the sins and blessings of the parents passed on to the children. This basic social unit becomes the primordial ground in which each of us works out our holiness.[3]

We are inundated with religious and political rhetoric about the family. But instead of helping us to integrate family life and faith, too often such talk impedes that process. And even after we have been exposed to ways of making the connections, the job of personal appropriation and interiorization remains. It is up to each person to glimpse the divine shining through daily experience, and to name the sacred times, places and people in our families.[4] Augustine spoke eloquently and movingly about the goal of life in terms of "returning home." He saw heaven as the wondrous fatherland from whence we came and whither we return. But we seldom think about this ultimate, eternal "home" in terms of the homes in which we were raised and in which we now live.

Theologians remind us of the "house churches" that developed in early Christianity.[5] At times the community gathered to break bread and remember the story of Jesus in the synagogue, but they often came together in homes to break bread and share a meal. Can the existence of these "house churches" lead us to reflect on our homes, our families and the relationships within them in light of the presence or absence of God? Wendy Wright reflects on the family's ways of being church.

> The family's ways of being Church have as much to do with inhabiting, with the co-penetration of bodies and hearts, with the dense fabric of human attachments, with busyness and business, with the labors of providing, with touching and being touched, with consciousness of the continuity and permanency of human existence.[6]

But Wright admits that her experience of family is only one of many, and cautions against the lie of seeing family exclusively in terms of a "nuclear" unit—an intact, heterosexual couple with children.

The universal call to holiness means just that—everybody gets a shot at it. We need to listen to the experiences of all kinds of families, to attend with love and compassion to the often agonizing struggles as well as the simple joys of troubled families, blended families, of single parents, divorced parents, of gay and lesbian couples, of single persons. All of us belong in some way to the world of families and all of us are called to recognize God in the specific, concrete circumstances of that existence.

The mystics can also serve as a resource for a contemporary spirituality. They use powerful and compelling language to speak about the heights and the depths of their intimate encounters with God. There is no reason why every baptized Christian should not recognize in the depths of her or his own daily experiences the same godly, care-filled presence. The profound desires, joys and contentments of family life; the enormous pain, agony and suffering of abuse, indifference, broken promises, and seemingly intractable breaches—this is the stuff of saint-making. Elizabeth Johnson captures the comprehensive scope of life in the Spirit.

In the sheer joy and pain of bearing, birthing, and rearing; in everyday, commonplace work; in living out freedom with its considered choices; in taking responsibility for our own life and its impact on others; in the depth of sin, despair, and emptiness; in accepting forgiveness and bestowing it; in the outbreak of joy and celebration; in befriending the stranger and caring for the truly helpless; in meeting limits and making peace with our finitude; in hoping against hope in the face of overwhelming oppression, suffering or death, or, in the absence of felt hope, in the sheer grit to go on—the mystery of God's Spirit, present and absent, is cogiven in every instance.[7]

The breadth of this vision calls us beyond our families and personal friends to wider communities, institutions and nations.

Institutions and Social Systems

There is a Hasidic saying that expresses succinctly the connection between God and the world. "Whoever says that the words of the Torah are one thing and the words of the world another must be regarded as a person who denies God."[8] The dualisms discussed in Part I have led us to divorce Christianity from political and economic affairs. A privatized spirituality too often leads to a stifled conscience. One test of a healthy spiritual life is the gradual expansion of our hearts to embrace the world. The expression of care and compassion within our families and in our relationships with friends and colleagues slowly and gradually extends its horizons to include those in the next town or country; those "others" who are different from us in race, sex, age and religion; and even those who have offended us or done us harm. Our love for the world cannot thrive without justice. Our love leads us to be concerned about how society is organized, how wealth, power, privileges, rights and responsibilities are distributed on every level—local, national and global. And the quality of our justice is tested by the ways in which we work to protect the poor and marginalized.

Finding God in institutions that seem mindless, heartless

and corrupt is no easy task. But we cannot live without institutions and if we do not work within them in positive, redeeming ways, they will continue as arms of dysfunction and oppression. A spirituality of everyday life involves noticing and upholding the positive forces in our institutions. It involves committing ourselves to the "life" of institutions in small and large ways. It may mean taking the risk of telling the truth. It may mean putting in a solid day's work and taking pride in our jobs—whatever they may be. It may mean weaning ourselves from an attitude that says, "I rip the company off, because the company rips me off."

A theology of the Holy Spirit reminds us that the reach of God has no bounds. There is no corner of the globe, no attitude or disposition, no atrocity that is absolutely sealed off against the light of the Spirit. In diverse ways, we are called upon to notice and support the loving and life-giving forces across our world. We are called upon to stand as firmly as we can against the complex and often elusive powers of darkness. And we have the mandate to contribute whenever and however we can, to the work of God in the world.

A spirituality of everyday life is located within the human situation and responds to it just as it is. It is designed to confer meaning on the totality of our lives and to heal the wounds resulting from the privation of the divine presence. Matthew's gospel provides both a literal and a symbolic starting point for us to participate in the work of the Spirit—in our families, on the job, in nature and in the entire world. "I was hungry and you gave me food. I was thirsty and you gave me drink. I was a stranger and you welcomed me" (25:35).

In their depth and authenticity, the entire Christian life and the whole cosmos are seen as the symbolic manifestation of God's love. In all the various situations of daily life, we are called upon to develop a sacramental imagination. In distinctive ways, all of us need to nurture our imaginative powers and take on the sacred task of noticing God-with-us. In a special way, Catholicism is a sacramental form of religion, that is, it has the capacity to see finite and relative things as media of the divine, thus endowing all of ordinary life with the possibilities and sanctity of divine creativity. Sacramental imagination is, therefore, a key resource for prophetic action in our world.[9]

As baptized Christians, we not only have the responsibility, but also the authority to view the world in this way. Growing in our awareness of, and ability to name, God's gift of Self to all the world will be accompanied by a new confidence that we are indeed loved by God; a new freedom to live in that love with more and more abandon; and a new delight in our common priesthood. Once we begin to notice the sacredness around us, we will be moved to exercise our priesthood, to raise up in oblation all the things and persons in our world. In his book, *An Offering of Uncles,* Anglican pastor and theologian, Robert Capon, refreshes our sense of the priesthood of Adam. He reminds us that we are the priests of creation, the offerers, the interceders, the seizers of its shape and agents of its history.

He also underscores the mutuality of the priestly task to spend our days raising up others.

> The beholding, the loving of my own being is somebody else's business, not mine. Persons were meant to enter into a dance of mutual oblation, a simultaneous offering of each other. The city, the web, history itself, is the tissue woven by such priestly acts.[10]

We do not stand alone. In community, the priestly "I" becomes the priestly "we." Through this priesthood, we actively participate in history by noticing the worldly face of God in its agony and in its joy, and by lifting up together, all of creation.

NOTES

1. Gerard Manley Hopkins, "God's Grandeur," *Poems and Prose of Gerard Manley Hopkins* (Baltimore: Penguin Books, 1953).

2. Some of the most penetrating analyses of the presence/absence of spirit in family life are to be found in contemporary fiction. A sampling of authors includes John Updike, Mary Gordon, Toni Morrison, Gloria Naylor, Amy Tan and Philip Roth.

3. Dolores R. Leckey offers a family approach to the Rule of St. Benedict in *The Ordinary Way: A Family Spirituality* (New York:

Crossroad, 1982). See also *Being Home: A Book of Meditations* by Gunilla Norris (New York: Bell Tower, 1991) and *Finding God at Home* by Ernest Boyer, Jr. (Harper: San Francisco, 1988 [1984]).

4. For example, Wendy M. Wright calls attention to the limitations of traditional metaphors such as "journey," "pilgrimage," or "battle," to describe the spiritual life. She develops the spatial metaphor of "dwelling," that she thinks will speak more truly to the majority of Christians whose call is to provide an environment in which to nurture family life. *Sacred Dwelling: A Spirituality of Family Life* (New York: Crossroad, 1989). See also Betsy Caprio and Thomas M. Hedbert, *Coming Home: A Handbook for Exploring the Sanctuary Within* (Mahwah, NJ: Paulist Press, 1986); and Thomas Howard, *Hallowed Be This House* (Wheaton, IL: Harold Shaw, 1978).

5. An example is the house of Prisca and Aquila, named by Paul as his co-workers (Romans 16:3–5).

6. Wendy Wright, *Sacred Dwelling*, p. 26.

7. Elizabeth Johnson, *She Who Is* (New York: Crossroad, 1992), p. 126.

8. Maurice Friedman, *A Heart of Wisdom: Religion and Human Wholeness* (Albany, New York: SUNY, 1992), p. 229.

9. Ibid., p. 255.

10. Robert Farrar Capon, *An Offering of Uncles: The Priesthood of Adam and the Shape of the World* (New York: Sheed and Ward, 1967), p. 115.

6

Towards a Spirituality of Work

Many Americans spend more than half their days and their lives working. Many more may feel as if they spend their *whole* lives working—except for a few hours of sleep, television or fishing. Perhaps only the Germans and the Japanese rival the American work ethic in terms of hours on the job. Yet it is surprisingly difficult to talk about work. Work experience itself is extremely diverse, and it means very different things to different people. Some common definitions of work include: "an activity that produces something of value for other persons,"[1] or "any activity, or expenditure of energy, that produces services and products of value to other people."[2]

Efforts are underway to broaden our understanding of work beyond public, salaried activity. By a rather circuitous route, the women's movement has led us to a new valuing of the work of child-rearing; keeping a household solvent, functioning and happy; volunteering. Robert Heilbroner writes:

> To write about the act of work is daunting because work is the focusing lens for so much of human experience. Work conjures up joy and despair, fulfillment and anesthesia, creativity and drudgery. It brings to mind the ideas of Marx and Aquinas, Freud and Benedict, Weber and Aristotle. It raises the most immediate and pressing issues of unemployment and discrimination, and the most perennial and persisting question of purpose and achievement. In a word, work is the inescapable starting point for all social inquiry—if only we knew where to start.[3]

In addition, people experience work differently. For some it is a way of making a living—whether this means barely surviving or surrounding oneself with all the luxuries money can buy.

For others it is a career that entails professional advancement, expanding competency and social standing. And for some few, work is seen as a calling, a valued and integral part of life that contributes to the public good.[4]

The story of work in the Garden of Eden includes both positive (Genesis 1) and negative (Genesis 3) aspects that have remained prominent throughout the Christian tradition. Work has been seen as both a blessing and a curse. Often the church has fought for and supported the dignity of work and the worker. The social encyclicals embody a long history of concern for the plight of the worker, and in the United States, the Catholic Church has been a prominent defender of trade unions.[5] But it is also fair to say that the Catholic community can do a great deal more to respond to the concerns of workers in the post-Vatican II church. In addition to defending the worker, how can the church assist Christians to experience work as an integral part of their spiritual life?[6]

It is in this context that we ask: How much do I really know about the work life of parishioners, colleagues, friends? What are the joys and problems associated with work? As workers, we ask ourselves: How do we balance home life and work life? How do we maintain a sense of dignity and self-respect on the job? How do we resist the temptation to callousness, selfishness, cynicism, despair? How do we hold to moral and religious values in the face of all sorts of challenges at work? What happens to people emotionally and spiritually when they compromise with certain important principles—start down the road of rationalization and self-justification? Understanding work in its ultimate horizon allows one to value work and connect it to the goodness of creation and with the creative aspects of one's life.

Can we enter realistically into the hopes and dreams of all workers in order to discover, celebrate, weep over, and struggle to bring life and dignity to, the world of work? We need to ask about how our own work can become an integral part of our spirituality and also about how we can struggle so that everyone's right to meaningful work can be honored.[7] Along with all the other aspects of everyday living, the experience of work has the potential to become a significant locus for the revelation of God. How can work—whether uplifting or boring—be an integral part of one's journey toward holiness? We present several perspectives intended to contribute to the ongoing dialogue with those who want to connect their lives of work with their lives in the Spirit.

I. WORK AS DARK NIGHT

For many people, work is a necessary evil, serving neither God nor the community, nor that which is noble in the human person.[8] In his book, *Working*, Studs Terkel says,

> This book, being about work, is, by its very nature, about violence—to the spirit as well as to the body.... It is about a search, too, for daily meaning as well as daily bread, for recognition as well as cash, for astonishment rather than torpor; in short, for a sort of life rather than a Monday through Friday sort of dying. Perhaps immortality, too, is part of the quest. To be remembered was the wish, spoken and unspoken, of the heroes and heroines of this book.[9]

The workers in Terkel's book do not find work pleasurable or satisfying on its own merits. They discover, rather, that work often fails to measure up to their own stature and hopes. One can quickly imagine their response to the idea of a spirituality of work: "I just need to figure out how to get through the day." "Why should I worry about having a spirituality of work when I just got laid off?" And one is right to reject a pious moralism (created by "armchair workers"?) that emphasizes only the personhood of the worker and ignores the kind of work the worker does.

The most frequent complaints against work are: lack of recognition; the nature of the job itself; being spied upon.[10] Often the elements that make work satisfying are absent: an intimate connection between the process of work and the finished product; a sense of control by the worker; opportunities for growth and development; integration of work with culture, leisure and the worker's entire mode of living.

The Christian tradition is not without resources when it

comes to the situation of those who hate their work, who find themselves trapped in difficult, demeaning and life-draining work situations, who are underemployed or unemployed. The cross stands as a central symbol in Christianity, shedding a ray of hope on a wide range of difficulties and suffering. Jesus was able to surrender to the reality of his existence in love and freedom. He didn't go kicking and screaming to his death, but embraced the suffering with dignity and redeeming love. Jesus' witness challenges us to choose to become vulnerable, to move through the dark night into conversion and new life.[11]

The invitation to continue this work of redemptive dying and rising has always been and remains at the heart of the Christian faith. This is not to suggest that we give up the fight for better work and better working conditions for ourselves and others. On the contrary, the experience of the dark night would be a shallow one if we turned our backs on our dreams or on the means at hand to improve our situation.

Suffering in and of itself is never anything but an evil to be eradicated. But life does bring suffering, and for many in our society today, that suffering is centered on meaningless work, fear of losing work, or the agony of being without work. When we are able to use aspects of the tradition such as the dark night in the context of work, we will experience ways in which such experiences can indeed contribute to our lives in the Spirit.

Constance Fitzgerald talks about extreme states of distress as "impasse." By "impasse" she means that there are no ways out of, no ways around, no possibilities, no rational escapes from, what imprisons one.[12] None of previously developed coping skills work, and as a result, one's self-image and sense of worth quickly evaporate. The ordinary means of support may be present, but the darkness prevents us from receiving them. Such extreme situations jolt and threaten us. One can choose to respond with passivity, cynicism and despair, or one can allow feelings of powerlessness to open the way to new, intuitive, symbolic and imaginative solutions.

In faith, one trusts that new possibilities can emerge *out of the darkness.* "The realization that there is no option but faith triggers a deep, silent, overpowering panic, that like a mighty underground river, threatens chaos and collapse."[13] Then darkness can beckon one to contemplation, to a new openness to the dark mystery of God. The grace of faith can lead one to see this limit situation as an invitation to let go and walk with Jesus to the cross. John of the Cross seems to be saying that we get out of this impasse by turning over one's powerlessness and frustration to the Spirit, thereby moving through rejection and despair to a new, transformed self-esteem, affirmation, compassion and solidarity.[14] The experience of impasse challenges us to become contemplatives, to allow our faith to transform experiences of disillusionment and hopelessness into hope and compassion, to turn our hearts of stone into hearts of flesh. An imaginative faith has the potential to turn our rage and anger into purifying tools that call forth a contemplative love for self and for the world that has abused us.

Another type of suffering related to work involves limiting one's sense of self to one narrow sector of life. Often our only sense of ourselves is our working selves—whether that be as mother, laborer or executive. Of course, one of the functions of work is that it does give a sense of self-esteem and community respect. But the spiritual tradition can help us see that whether I am able to work in the more formal sense or not, I am still "someone" in God's eyes and, one hopes, in others' eyes and in my own. It is possible to change one's self-perception from "I am a worker," to "I am someone who sometimes works," or to "I am someone who happens to be out of work."[15]

II. WORK AND CREATION[16]

To begin, we see work as a part of a creation that is intrinsically good. Unfortunately, work has been yet another victim of our tendency to ghettoize the holy—limiting it to deserts, caves, monasteries, convents, churches and rectories.[17] But of course the locus of God's revealing Self-gift is not so restricted, and it is time for us to wake up to the potential holiness of the office, the union meeting, city streets, the classroom and the assembly line.

In *One Minute Wisdom*, Anthony de Mello relates the following conversation:

> —Said the Master to the businessman: "As the fish perishes on dry land, so you perish when you get entangled in the world. The fish must return to the water, you must return to solitude."
>
> —The businessman was aghast. "Must I give up my business and go into the monastery?"
>
> —"No, no. Hold onto your business and go into your heart."[18]

As a church, we have begun to open ourselves in ways that allow God to be present in all aspects of our existence. But we still have miles to go before we become leaders in the commitment to Christian solidarity with the problems of today's world of work. Our *primary* sense of being in and for the world must be Christian presence and behavior at home, in medical labs, in factories, department stores, courtrooms, schools and corporate boardrooms, *not* parochial peace and justice committees.

In the creation account in Genesis, we read that God did not covet the role of creator in an exclusive sense, but rather invited humanity to participate in, and take responsibility for, the ongoing creation of the world (Gen 2:5–25). Along with love and art and action for justice, work is a primary locus in which we share in God's creative life. Human creativity in all its wonderful diversity does not compete with God's creative power but participates in, fulfills, and completes it.

Physics teaches us about the dynamic character of the universe. And while stars and galaxies move inexorably along their paths, culture is shaped by the creative dynamism of productive, human energies. As the breath of the spirit moved over the watery chaos in the creation story, so too does human work have the potential to bring order and beauty out of the chaos that threatens us on many sides.[19]

The creative aspect of work is easier to grasp in some occupations than in others. Obvious candidates include producing art or music; developing grace and athletic prowess in the human body; raising children; building buildings or sculpting gardens. When this work is motivated by an active love for the world, by a desire to enhance its quality of life, it is easy to see a reflection of God's creative power. But work that is drudgery poses a stiffer challenge and calls for a different response.

Growth in Self-Knowledge

Work can be a place in which I discover myself as well as prove myself. Work can become an arena in which one becomes a good person, in which one practices and gains a certain ease in being virtuous, thereby becoming holy. We often fail to see that the challenges, trials, and joys of work are part of the essence of the spiritual life. The very nature of work offers daily opportunities for spiritual growth. The locus of the spiritual life cannot be alongside of or parallel to the activities of our lives. Nor can we afford any longer to limit the spiritual life to private prayer, or retreats, or church on Sunday. Spending oneself to make a good product, dealing honestly with disappointment or humiliation, or taking risks to be honest or truthful—this is the very stuff of the spiritual life.

As Christians, we believe that persons are made in the image and likeness of God. One aspect of God's image is creative activity, and the Christian story invites believers to be like God in this creative dimension.[20] Workers may balk at the suggestion that work is creative but, as we have seen above, work that is honest and performed with integrity is one vehicle through which we cooperate with God to build up a broken and struggling world. Work, and the sense we have of ourselves, take on a new dignity when we see it as doing God's work rather than simply working for God. God bestows new dignity on the human race with this invitation to continue to bring about the kingdom now, in this world. Jesus brought the kingdom to the world by engaging in rather ordinary, mundane work and he often used stories about work to convey his message. He engaged in work with a directness and unassuming simplicity that can serve as a model for those workers who profess to follow in his footsteps.

Too often we shy away from the fullness and the success of work, because we mistakenly see our work in competition with the work of God.[21] Rather than seeking success in order to make a better world and to praise God, we get nervous about seeking success, thinking that success and holiness are inversely proportionate or unrelated. How skewed is such a view that leads Christians to undervalue their work or to fall short of the total commitment necessary to bring about the kingdom of God on earth! The incarnation means nothing if it does not mean that human activity is "God's business." Work performed with integrity is a sign of God's greatness. The triumphs of a talented human race, executed in love, do nothing but enhance God's glory before all the world.

III. WORK AND COMMUNITY

A sense of community is both a prerequisite and an outcome of meaningful work. Growth in one's ability to situate work in a larger context also helps overcome the split between work and family, between public and private domains. The fruits of work allow one to provide for one's family shelter, nourishment, education and opportunites for growth and development. Even difficult work that does not seem intrinsically valuable can become tolerable and take on meaning when it is seen as part of the gesture of love toward family and friends.

Beyond one's intimate circle, the road of spirituality leads to consciousness and care of ever wider community groups. For example, one may choose to live a simple lifestyle as both a material and symbolic gesture toward those in the world who lack basic necessities. Work can also become religiously meaningful when one realizes that the goods of the earth belong to the people of the earth and are not "mine" in a possessive sense. We are gifted by God with all manner of wonderful things and asked to reverence and care for them as faithful stewards, not as greedy consumers.

One's awareness of the larger community can also be a catalyst for paying attention to the conditions and results of work. One may have to confront the status quo, leading to risky decisions such as supporting worker organizations in order to ensure justice and safety on the job or lobbying to change legislation that puts workers in oppressive and powerless positions, or fighting to change the kind of work that destroys the environment. Some will be called upon to help workers when unemployed, or to train persons for new jobs, or to locate or create new positions as the market economy changes drastically from products to service. Do we have the courage to work to change structures, to dream of a time when "the submission and discipline of work might become the free act of obedience of all members of society to their own purposes, not to those of a small minority"? Can we work to transform social subordination to social responsibility?[22]

As a nation, we have become acutely aware that our connections to others are no longer limited to family or neighborhood. Work in any part of the world now often has swift and direct effects on work in far distant corners of the globe. Many of our immediate problems with work are connected to this global reality. But whether our work is odious or glorious; whether done at home, in the office, in a mine or on an assembly line, it is part of this larger global scene in which we are called to transform the world. We court disaster if we persist in seeing our work in splendid isolation from the rest of the world. The challenge is to see ourselves and our work from "inside" this global community and to work at solutions from this pespective rather than from an exclusively adversarial position.

IV. SPIRITUALITY OF THE PRESENT MOMENT

For many Christians work takes on spiritual significance when they choose to live in the present moment, to notice and value God working there, and to offer a loving response in a full and integral way.[23] The Greeks call this kind of moment *kairos,* distinguishing it from *chronos,* the moment that is simply part of the chain of time that marches on willy-nilly with the movement of hands on a clock. *Kairos* is not just time passing, but time that is perceived as significant and demanding of response. In this kind of time, persons recognize the pregnant quality of both ordinary and extraordinary work events and do not let them slip through their fingers.

This model of a spirituality of work demands a discipline that keeps one focused on what is present *now*. It involves paying reverent attention to the person or the task at hand and doing the job right. Gradually we are learning that to be a good plumber, truck driver, nurse, or janitor is the way to be a good Christian. The heart of Christian spirituality is wherever we are in the world, not in the church building. The incarnation is the theological bedrock upon which to build such a spirituality of work. Christian spirituality is always enfleshed in the totality of our daily existence.

Such a spirituality also means not spending the day wishing I were somewhere else, constantly expending energy resisting the urge to escape. In difficult situations, one is called upon to trust that one can make some sense of the situation, work to create alternatives, and be ready to move on if and when the opportunity presents itself.

Persons who already see their work as a major aspect of their spirituality speak about how they apply the tenets and values of Christianity in the workplace. They take several key principles of the Christian life—those that are both simple and profound—and try to live by them in the workplace. Some speak about respect for others because they are made in God's image. They put into practice the golden rule to do unto others as you would have them do unto you. These Christians have also interiorized Jesus' way of forgiveness and so are able to offer the forgiving word to colleagues. They imitate Jesus' way of humility, keeping a rein on the penchant to go about blaming others for the millions of hurts with which the workplace is filled. They are careful to deal with colleagues in a loving way, especially when they have to be the bearer of bad news about performance or termination of employment.

This way is available to all persons, but it is not easy. Maintaining daily attention, patience, forgiveness, cooperation, generosity and a joyful countenance can be an enormous challenge. It is so much easier to close oneself off from others, to become cynical and mistrusting, to diminish coworkers instead of lifting them up because they are valuable in God's sight and therefore in our own. It takes commitment to perdure in this "way" for the long haul of our work lives. But the fruits of holiness can come to full flower through such practice.

Another aspect to a spirituality of work is the application of Christian ethical principles, which can be a difficult road to travel when there is an absence of a moral sense or the acceptance of unethical business practices. The marketplace often chooses efficiency over moral standards. One is confronted not only with personal greed, but systemic problems that are elusive and extremely difficult to correct. It is a tragedy when Christians are left to face these difficulties alone without the support of the believing community or the benefit of a tradition that has grappled since its beginnings with ethical issues; with the development of the virtues of courage, peace, justice, honesty; and with the formation of conscience. Alone the burden is impossible. Together we find glimmers of hope as even small pieces of the solution emerge out of prayerful reflection on the issues.

V. THEOLOGICAL REFLECTION ON WORK

Until now, we have focused on interior dispositions, ways of conducting oneself in the work place, and on making connections between work and one's spiritual life. All of these can be enhanced through the practice of theological reflection—an activity that takes place ideally in a group setting.[24] A major impetus for such gatherings has been the success of the base communities in Central and South America described by liberation theologians.[25] Many Christians in North America have experienced the beginning stages of such reflection in Bible study and renewal groups across the country.

The initiative for such groups can come from parish leaders or, ideally, from the grass roots believing community itself. Groups can be structured in any number of ways—neighbors in a local area or persons who do a certain kind of work, e.g., homemakers, assembly workers at a local plant, executives, insurance brokers, beauticians, artists. The process is simple. Members of the group begin to get in touch with and talk about what their work is like—its problems, its joys, its possibilities. Each person focuses on feelings as well as ideas, and participants are encouraged to listen and refrain from making quick judgments about the situation presented. Then, in a simple and reverent way, the group begins to reflect on the work experience in light of their broader life experience and the Christian message—the good news of the gospel and the ways in which Jesus lived with and for others.

In an open and prayerful setting, the group members attend to the ways in which the Spirit might shed light on their experience and understanding of work, on its difficulties and on the solutions that are revealed as a result of such dialogue. It is perhaps the best way to stay grounded in the actual experience of work, to experience the love and care of a Christian community, and to be led in the ways of the Spirit in regard to that work.

Finally, a word about keeping ourselves honest about work. The stereotypes—"work is a drag," and "work is all"—are alive and well and everywhere among us. Persons need to identify their particular illusions about work and move toward letting them go. One such illusion is that work is all bad, narrowly utilitarian, a curse, something we have to endure until the weekend, the vacation, or retirement. Joseph Pearce describes it well.

> The American work week is posited between "Gloomy Monday" and "Thank God it's Friday," a strange polarity indicating a majority of misery amidst brief respites... Bumper stickers on automobiles announce a wide variety of "I'd rather be's": "I'd rather be skiing, swimming, horseback riding, surfing..."—anything, apparently, other than what one is doing.[26]

One source of this negative attitude is the teaching that work is a punishment for sin. Another source is the human desire to focus on the negative side of things. But one aspect of the "work is a drag" mentality is that quite often it is simply true. And humor is often a very good way to deal with the situation creatively. But for most of us that is only part of the picture.

Another illusion holds that work encompasses the totality of existence, the sole source of identity, health and salvation. Those prone to a "work is all" mentality may have prestigious, challenging and lucrative work that threatens to become an idol, an all-consuming absolute that feeds the ego and obscures the rest of life. Others may focus on work because they do not want to face the rest of their lives.

But work is not just a drain and it was not meant to become an absolute. It may be a useful exercise for those who are employed to imagine being without work. What if there were no office to go to, no garbage to pick up, no house to clean, no children to rear, no cars to make? We need to acknowledge the many positive fruits and benefits of work. Good work of any kind is the locus of innumerable blessings and satisfactions—something constructive to do with our time; personal identity and fulfillment; self-esteem; a sense of belonging to society; source of support; sense of achievement; avenue of personal and communal growth.

One of the hallmarks of the spiritual life is a willingness to see and embrace life in its totality. Part of the spiritual journey involves devising ways to keep oneself honest, to ward off illusions that tempt us on a daily basis. The Christian life invites us in many and diverse ways to create another picture of work—one which includes its giftedness as well as its suffering, its limitations as well as its satisfactions. Is it possible to grow in freedom with regard to work, even to enjoy the process of work? Might we ever be able to "play" at work?[27]

Conclusion

No doubt you, the reader, can add your own thoughts to this conversation about work. Ultimately, as Christians, we have to ask critically whether our values hinder or reinforce the unequal, exploitative and oppressive distribution of work. Our vision of work must include everyone—from the poorest to the most affluent in our society. Any authentic spirituality of work will uncover paths of hope, leading to solidarity among all workers. It will point to work as a central way of fulfilling our religious responsibilities toward society, thus allowing us to integrate that aspect of our lives into our spirituality.

Such a spirituality must also deal forthrightly with the complexity, diversity, ambiguity and inequity of the experience and meaning of work on personal, ecclesial and societal levels. A Christian spirituality of work, grounded in the mysteries of incarnation, death and resurrection will overcome the bifurcation of sacred and secular and proclaim the oneness and the goodness of creation and our work in it.

As Christians we have a responsibility to attend to our lives of work. Not only must we read articles and become more aware of the intersection of work and spirituality, but we must let our desire for universal holiness spur our imaginations to creative action on behalf of all workers. We can allow ourselves to become genuinely curious about work and ask people about it. We can listen to stories about work, visit people at work, ask how the faith community can be of assistance to those who work.

Do we, as a Christian community, place ourselves in service to workers and work? Do we preach about the rewards of work and its benefits?[28] Do we talk about earning money as a good? Do we search for ways to weep over the pain of work, express gratitude for it, and celebrate its goodness in our lives? We are called upon to join others in society who are already attentive to ways to improve the quality of work and its effects on the world and its environment. We can lend our intelligence and conviction to the cause of equality, just wages, and humane working conditions. We can emulate those persons who have been particularly successful at integrating work and the spiritual life.

What if all the enormous energies of persons in the church were understood, not in the utilitarian mode so common in our society, but as a real contribution to the development of the kingdom of God? What if the act of work, whatever its nature, were seen as a creative act in union with the Creator, that actually builds up the earth and helps form a new human family? What if all this toil and labor were viewed as very concrete ways to continue the redemptive activity of Jesus, a specific mode of dying and rising with him? What if the spiritual lives of millions of Christians were expanded to include their whole lives, including the daily round of work?[29] What if?

NOTES

1. Richard Hall, *Dimensions of Work* (Beverly Hills, CA: Sage Publications, 1986), p. 11.

2. Mary Frank Fox and Sharlene Hesse-Biber, *Women at Work* (Palo Alto, CA: Mayfield Publishing Company, 1984), p. 2.

3. Robert L. Heilbroner, *The Act of Work* (Washington, D.C.: Library of Congress, 1985), p. 9.

4. See Robert Bellah et al., *Habits of the Heart* (Berkeley, CA: University of California Press, 1985), p. 66.

5. The social encyclicals frequently address the issue of work in positive ways, e.g., *Rerum novarum/1891* and *Populorum progressio/1967* point to particular evils in the workplace, while *On Human Work/1981* offers a broader theology of work.

6. See Eric Steven Dale, *Bringing Heaven Down to Earth: A Practical Spirituality of Work* (New York: Peter Lang, 1991); William E. Diehl, *The Monday Connection* (San Francisco: Harper and Row, 1991); John C. Haughey, *Converting 9 to 5: A Spirituality of Daily Work* (New York: Crossroad, 1989); Joe Holland, *Creative Communion: Toward A Spirituality of Work* (Mahwah, NJ: Paulist Press, 1989); Gregory F. Augustine Pierce, ed., *Of Human Hands: A Reader in the Spirituality of Work* (Minneapolis: Augsburg Press, 1991); Douglas Steere, *Work and Contemplation* (New York: Harper & Row, 1957); Miroslav Volf, *Work in the Spirit: Toward A Theology of Work* (New York: Oxford University Press, 1991); *Weavings* 8(Jan–Feb 1993), entire issue is on work.

7. The National Center for the Laity has made many significant contributions to this topic. Information about their newsletter, *Initiatives*, can be obtained from William Droel at 1 E. Superior St. #311, Chicago, IL 60611.

8. Dorothy Soelle uncovers the many aspects of alienated work in the image of the treadmill. *To Work and To Love: A Theology of Creation.* Philadelphia: Fortress, 1984, pp. 55f.

9. Studs Terkel, *Working* (New York: Pantheon Books, 1972).

10. Ibid., p. xviii.

11. See Constance Fitzgerald, "Impasse and Dark Night" in *Women's Spirituality,* ed. Joann Wolski Conn (New York: Paulist Press, 1986), pp. 287–311.

12. Ibid., p. 288.

13. Ibid., p. 297-98.

14. Ibid.

15. James E. Dittes, *When Work Goes Sour* (Louisville, KY: Westminster Press, 1988), p. 103.

16. See Joan Chittister, "Work: Participation in Creation," *Weavings* 8(January/February, 1993): 1–9.

17. See Ed Marciniak, "Toward a Catholic Work Ethic," *Origins* 17 (1988): 634.

18. Anthony de Mello, *One Minute Wisdom* (Garden City, NY: Doubleday, 1986), p. 13. Cited in Marciniak, p. 634.

19. Soelle, *To Work and To Love*, p. 38.

20. See Matthew Fox, *Original Blessing* (Santa Fe, NM: Bear and Company, 1983) pp. 178f.

21. See Lothar Schneider, "The Spirituality of Work," *Social Justice Review* 78 (May-June, 1987): 96–99.

22. Heilbroner, *The Act of Work*, p. 24.

23. See Elizabeth Dreyer et al., "The Christian in the Workplace: Four Reflections," *New Theology Review* 2(May 1989): 40–52.

24. See Sisters of Mercy of the Union, *The Communal Search for Truth*, 1988.

25. See Marcello Azevedo, *Basic Ecclesial Communities in Brazil* (Washington, D.C.: Georgetown University Press, 1987).

26. Joseph Chilton Pearce, "Reaping the Whirlwind," *Darshan: Honoring Work* 32 (November 1989), p. 9.

27. Dittes, *When Work Goes Sour*, p. 88.

28. See Marjorie Procter-Smith, "Worship, the World and Work", an essay on the meaning of the "work" that is liturgy. *Liturgy* 6(1987): 61–65. Also Robert W. Hovda, "The Amen Corner: A Labor Day Reflection on Worship and Work." *Worship* 61 (1987): 454–460.

29. Alred Hennelly, "A Spirituality of Work," in *On Human Work* (Washington, D.C.: USCC, 1982), p. 34.

Ministry in the Marketplace

Vatican II engendered a widespread examination of the church's ministry. As the church struggled to respond to the needs of the late twentieth century, the practice of ministry leaped ahead of reflection on it. But as the church changed in its self-perception, it became clear that our ideas about ministry should change as well, emerging from the very nature of the church itself. We began to ask: Should ministry continue to refer only to the work of clergy and other professionals serving the church? Or should we see it as an essential element of the whole Christian community, as central to the baptismal covenant and therefore a pivotal aspect of every Christian's life?[1] In this chapter, I will speak about this wider ministry under the following headings: recent theological discussions about ministry; ministry in the marketplace; and some qualities of a future renewed ministry.

I. RECENT THEOLOGICAL DISCUSSION[2]

As we have seen, Vatican II served as a catalyst for the church to embrace new attitudes toward the world, to bring forth the Holy Spirit from the wings, to recover the centrality of baptism and to encourage the laity to take their rightful place in the church. As a consequence, we realized that reigning ideas about service in the faith community and the world were inadequate and required a far-reaching overhaul.

Over the past fifty years, the study of ministry has been dominated by teachers of pastoral care.[3] But recently, scholars from other branches of theology have undertaken systematic reflections on ministry as well. We are beginning to realize that theology and ministry go hand in hand. Theology will be changed as a result of theologians' reflective attention to today's ministerial praxis. And, in turn, ministry will be influenced by theological work that searches for historical antecedents, using the tradition as a critical tool in renewing the practice of ministry in the church.[4] One impetus for this reanimated theological discussion is recent ecumenical dialogue in the World Council of Churches between Protestant and Catholic churches, and among other groups in search of union. A surprising amount of common theological understanding about ministry is emerging from these efforts.[5]

And on the practical level, we have witnessed a burgeoning of lay ministries since Vatican II. Lay interest in theology and ministry, as well as a shortage of ordained clergy, are factors contributing to this growth. Some in the church no longer consider sacramental ministry as the primary or only "real" ministry. Also acknowledged as legitimate ministers are religious educators, pastoral counsellors, home visitors, eucharistic ministers, musicians, parish administrators, teachers, hosts and hostesses, and bookkeepers.

But what about the work that is done everyday, throughout the world, by ordinary baptized Christians? Are we to understand such engagement in the world as a form of ministry, vital to both church and society? And if so, how should we ground this understanding of ministry theologically? Our growing awareness of, and appreciation for, the many gifts in the community, and the knowledge that many of those gifts remain untapped, are forcing us to reexamine our categories. To begin, let us identify some of the major questions and preoccupations of recent theologies of ministry. Most of these theologians see their work as very necessary at this time, and as generally supportive of new ministries. Yet they are also tentative, probing, knowing that a great deal more experience is needed.

1. Almost every author acknowledges a crisis in ministry, a crisis that is seen as an opportunity, and for some a mandate, to reflect theologically on the church's mission. This crisis is caused, in part, by the church's new and open attitude toward society and culture. In the wake of this openness has come confusion about many ecclesial issues, primary among them being

the substance of ministry and the identity of the minister. Questions have arisen about how effective ministry has been in its task of calling attention to the transcendent in today's world; about how well the church understands and responds to the real needs of today's people; about the tension between the laity and the clergy; about the shortage of ordained clergy, and about the real pain and suffering that is being experienced by many in the church as a result of these changes.

2. In their historical analyses, most theologians have traced a narrowing trend in the nature and functions of ministry from the early years of Christianity to the present. Some point to one event or period as more significant than another, but most agree that in the beginning, a minister arose out of a given community of believers and was intimately related to that community. Gradually this connection was weakened and in the medieval period disappeared altogether. The concept of the ministerial power of the Spirit operating in and through a community became, instead, that of the personal power of an officeholder to celebrate eucharist. We are groping mightily to reverse that trend and move to a broader understanding of ministry.

3. Vatican II signalled a change of emphasis from the cultic to the diaconal in its understanding of ministry.[6] Many of the authors in our sample (Tavard and Macquarrie being exceptions) agree with the direction set by Hans Küng in *The Church*, that emphasizes charism over office.[7] The conviction that ministry must be reconnected in a primary way with the needs of people, has led to the position that a variety of gifts is required in order to respond to the diversities of needs in the world. Authors do not want to oppose ministry as charism to ministry as office but, rather, in view of our past and present situations, they see the need to emphasize the charismatic dimension.

4. Theologians now realize that a theology of ministry cannot stand on its own, but must be placed in a much larger theological context, that includes history, anthropology, pneumatology, christology, ecclesiology, biblical studies, a theology of grace, and eschatology. In fact, one must take not only the theological sciences into consideration, but also broader inquiries by historians, culture analysts, psychologists and sociologists. This "secular" information cannot be placed in some "theological storm-

free zone" (to use Schillebeeckx's phrase), that will result in a "business-as-usual" ministry that fails in significant ways to give meaning to, and re-present, the presence of God in our time.[8]

A narrow, parochial approach to ministry disregards our experience, runs the risk of turning grace into magic, and ignores the theological ramifications of the incarnation.

Let us move now to something *not* present in this literature in any developed way—a theology of what I call "ministry in the marketplace." This is a view of ministry that is based in baptism and that takes account of one's daily involvement in culture and society as potentially religious activities.

II. MINISTRY IN THE MARKETPLACE

Ministry in the marketplace is that which takes place wherever people find themselves—on the job, at home, at leisure. Many Catholics today are beginning to search for ways to connect what they do for forty, fifty and even sixty hours a week with their spirituality. In the regional consultations that took place in this country in preparation for the 1987 Synod on the Laity, this issue came up repeatedly, even though often in a vague way. People have heard about this understanding of ministry and sense in some way that it is important, but are not clear about what it means. Bob Kinast, in a report on these consultations writes:

> As with the spiritual life, these faithful recognize that ministry includes secular activity, but they are not sure what this means or how to accomplish it. Most often they mention social services and charitable activities. Almost never are efforts toward structural change cited or opportunities to influence society through work, political involvement or civic organizations.[9]

Some of the reasons for this are obvious. Few of those writing on ministry are employed full-time at a bank or a record store, or selling insurance, or raising children, and so do not have the benefit of that kind of experience and the light that is shed on it by Christian commitment. Second, the focus on formal, ordained ministry has been so exclusive for so long, that few of us know how to think in other categories. In addition, the growing number of laity in formal ministry has tended to keep us in this mindset. Third, formal ministry is a more obvious kind of ministry and therefore easier to discuss. It is more circumscribed and identifiable and has more set structures than ministry in the marketplace. The pluriformity of the latter can be overwhelming and resist efforts at systematization.

Finally, the radical disjuncture we have known between sacred and secular makes the marketplace an unlikely place to look for the activities and fruits of the church's ministry—even though the church has said that this is the special realm of the laity.[10] An attitude of superiority is often betrayed when persons speak of the differences between the ministries of laity and clergy as "higher" and "lower"; or "good" and "better."[11] There is also the suggestion that since the ordained ministry is the most visible form of Christian service, we need simply to talk about it, since it applies automatically to all other kinds of service in the church.[12] Indeed, the result of such writing is the creation of an invisible ministry, a ministry that is not given its proper valuation in the church's life—at least as we express it verbally. David Power captures the tone of ambiguity still present in our thinking about ministry:

> On the bottom rung, the one that is most down to earth, there is the daily Christian involvement in temporal affairs, called by the rather generic term of "witness," but obviously involving much sweat and tears if a person is to take unfailing cognizance of the gospel in all things. It is this which is rather constantly and consistently pointed to in magisterial documents on service and ministry as that which constitutes the basic function of lay Christians and the most important part of their Christian service, rendered in the name and in the love of Christ. In one mouth, this can sound like an admonition to the laity to keep to their place. In another, it is a cry of anguish, lest Christ be absent from the affairs of the world.[13]

Mindful of these difficulties, let us launch out into these

uncharted waters in order to continue the conversation about ministry and to offer a new viewpoint.

Ministry as Response to the Needs of the World

We are true to the model of Jesus to the extent that we attend with care and reverence to our own time with its joys, challenges, opportunities, problems, suffering, and injustices. Since ministry is essentially a response to need, being a minister involves discerning what these needs are, and listening and responding to them in the light of the gospel. This means that nothing, *a priori*, is excluded from the realm of ministry. It includes the needs of economics, politics, social structures, our intellectual and affective life, business, ecology, personal relationships, and medicine as well as explicitly religious needs. Ministry means nurturing life and goodness and combatting death and evil in any of these spheres.

In a recent interview, Old Testament scholar, Walter Brueggemann says that when we hear the word "Yahweh," we should hear justice, righteousness, and faithfulness. He underlines the connection between religion and public policies. Commenting on Jeremiah 22 he says, "Caring for the poor and the needy is the act of knowing God...Prophetic faith insists that human choice and human policy-making are of decisive importance."[14]

The existence of the sacred/profane dualism noted above, interferes with this conception of ministry. An easy (and I would add, grossly inadequate) solution we have often espoused is to assign "secular" activity to the laity and "sacred" activity to the clergy, or to hold that the clergy minister to the Christian community and the laity minister to the world. While a fully satisfying response to this difficulty may be elusive, any solution must take seriously the effect of creation and incarnation upon all of existence. Bernard Cooke speaks to this issue: "If anything is new in our present situation it is the realization in the church that the matter cannot be solved authentically by divorcing Christianity and 'the secular.' This realization has been and is one of the most powerful influences in forcing a reconsideration of Christian ministry."[15]

Since ministry is a response to the needs of the world, we need to distinguish at least two different kinds of needs. One is the need that is overtly oriented toward the transcendent. There is an openness to God in the human person that strains toward the transcendent whether we are conscious of it or not. A second kind of need is less overtly religious and has to do with becoming fully human, that is, the ability to live in freedom and dignity, with access to food, housing, work and education. The first need requires hearing about God and discovering how God is present in one's life. The second need involves things like fighting for a just wage, or lobbying to save our diminishing rain forests. God's unbounded, unconditional love for the world includes both the desire that God be known and loved and that we live as full human beings.

The Role of Intention

One needs as well to consider the role of intention. What are the reasons behind our daily actions? What is moving the owner of a business to be color blind in hiring employees? James Fenhagen speaks eloquently to this issue.[16] He says that if we have a vision of ministry that encompasses all of life and empowers us to bear witness to the presence of Christ at every point of existence, then our being, our actions and our words can be an expression of ministry. Ministry is the term used to describe the ways in which we live out the implications of our baptism. If the meaning of who we are and what we do is connected with the grace of Christ, then that being and doing becomes ministerial. It involves what we understand to be the ultimate purpose and meaning of our lives.

Until we begin to speak of ministry as something normative for everyone in the church, it will continue to be seen only as something that is highly specialized and "churchy" in connotation.[17] The Spirit's power in the community enables every baptized person to hear and respond to this call to nurture life.

Ministry as Public

If we choose to embrace this broader "ministry in the marketplace," we need to address the issue of publicness. Thomas O'Meara names the public character of ministry as one of its six major characteristics. He says:

> When we say ministry is public, we mean that the ministry normally takes on a visible and public form in words and deeds....The communication of the Gospel has not been done mainly through uncertain signs, such as justice in commerce or casual neighborliness although these may be part of Christian life.[18]

Official public ministry is extremely important not only for its concrete accomplishments, but also for its symbolic value in the community. I agree strongly that the ministry that is visible, and clearly interpreted as the gift and fruit of the grace of Christ, is important—though not when it obscures the ministry of justice in commerce or casual neighborliness.

The intent of an idea like "ministry in the marketplace" is not to diminish the extensive public ministries of the church— from Catholic Charities to church sponsored relief programs too numerous to mention. All such ministries give overt witness to the Spirit of God active in the world. What is needed, I believe, is a complementary analysis of how we are to understand actions that are ministry but not in this public sense.

Our earlier discussion of intention and meaning in chapter 2 is relevant here. One thing that makes action ministry is that we *intend* it as such, that is, as related to our faith commitment. When persons see their everyday, ordinary lives as the locus of their spiritual journey, then the actions of those lives take on a heightened meaning. But let us ask a further question: How important is it that persons who are the beneficiaries of ministry *know* what the motivation behind the action is? In a similar vein, Bernard Cooke raises the question: "What difference does it make whether a certain agent of salvation or a certain course of saving action is 'official'?"[19] In some situations, action for the good of others may cause an overt inquiry: Why are you doing this for me? Or, we have all had the experience of realizing, after-the-fact, that we have been the beneficiaries of kind-nesses from family or friends whose motivation was the love of God. Such a discovery can become a catalyst for our own faith renewal and commitment to service. In more intimate relation-ships, it frequently becomes known that the actions of a friend or family member do indeed flow from their religious commit-ments.

But in the interest of a more universal ministry, we need to ask to what extent it should be a goal of ministry to tell people about our motivations? Should it be of primary or ultimate sig-nificance, or rather a hope, a desire that can be celebrated when given? At the least, we should examine the reasons behind any compulsion to divulge our motives uninvited. Perhaps too much of our ministry in the past has been tainted with arrogance and self-aggrandizement in this regard. As we become attuned to the mysteriousness of God's action, we may become free from worrying about whether people know why we are acting and free to concentrate on making this planet a bet-ter place to live for all people.

In support of giving full value to what we may call "anony-mous ministry," I point to two stories from the New Testament. The first is the story of the Good Samaritan (Luke 10:25–37). The passage explains the great commandment: Love God and love your neighbor. But in the story, there is no talk of God. Rather the story answers the question at the heart of ministry—who is my neighbor? We also note that the one who proves to be neighbor is not the one we might expect to perform well because of office. Rather, it is the Samaritan *who is moved to pity,* and *who shows the wounded man kindness.* The Good Samaritan is also a risk-taker. He disdains convention for a high-er good, opening himself to possible harsh criticism from his peers who want to preserve the status quo. All of us can name persons who act similarly. Walter Brueggemann notes his amazement "at the number of people in local communities who run enormous risks based on questions of justice and never get any publicity but get their share of abuse."[20]

The second story is part of Matthew's eschatological dis-course in chapter 25:31–46. At the separation of the sheep and the goats at the end of time, the Son of man explains why the sheep are to enter into the kingdom. They fed the hungry, gave drink to the thirsty, clothed the naked, etc. *But they did not even know they had done this.* And the well-known reply, "anything you did for one of my children here, however humble, you did for me." These stories challenge us to acknowledge, value and celebrate all kinds of ministry—the ministry that is publicly named, the ministry that is named in the heart of the minister, but not by the beneficiaries, and even the ministry that is not so named by the ministers themselves.

III. A FUTURE RENEWED MINISTRY

Any assessment of ministry needs to respond to the following questions. Does it effectively enhance awareness in this present culture of the power and love of God in a form that has promise for human beings as they perceive reality?[21] What can we do to further human history, that is, to alleviate the oppression and suffering of people and foster the movement toward freedom and dignity?[22] In order to respond affirmatively to these questions for our own time, we will need to keep the following issues and questions before us.

The Common Priesthood of the People of God

There is a frequently voiced desire to return to an earlier understanding of priesthood as it was applied to the whole Christian people.[23] This desire for a communal focus is supported by recent discussions on the destructive aspects of what some consider to be rampant individualism in the United States.[24] If anything, Christianity is a community affair, and in our time there is a longing to recover this charism. Authentic ministry emerges out of the community and not vice versa. We endeavor to reestablish this community connection.

In addition to reestablishing links between official ministry and the community, all baptized Christians are called to awareness of their individual and corporate priesthood. How can we encourage all Christians to translate their own faith into whatever course of service seems desirable? What kind of education/invitation should be extended? What things would motivate us to enhance our sense of being ministers wherever we find ourselves? What tools do we need in order to do this? Most importantly, how can we communicate the good news that many of the actions in the community already provide sterling examples of ministry—simply unrecognized because of the narrow parameters we have placed around ministry?[25]

Uncovering God's Presence

A second characteristic of a renewed ministry involves changing some of our language and understanding about ministry so that it more accurately reflects its true reality. Too many theologians discussing ministry use verbs like "bringing," "offering," "giving," "mediating," "helping," even "confronting" the world with God's power. Within a certain important but limited horizon this kind of language has a place—we need to continue to tell the story of God's saving love in Christ—but it does not get at the deepest reaches of the reality of ministry, and in fact may belie presuppositions that are inimical to it.

The truth to keep before us as ministers in the cosmos is that God is already in the world in more ways and more intimately than we can imagine. Granted, we also abuse, reject and are blinded to this presence, but this failure cannot obliterate the primary task of ministry which is to "uncover," "evoke," or "re-present" the presence of God. There is a profound sense in which talk of "bringing God to the world" smacks of an arrogance too bold to contemplate. From this vantage point, then, an important task of the minister is *to see*—not only needs of people, but ways in which grace is present in our world. The ability to recognize, name, affirm and celebrate goodness is an unparalleled gift of ministry—a gift that can be used to build up the people and give glory to God.

Belonging to the World

We have spoken at length about the need for Christians to experience themselves as part of, rather than as over against, the world. One cannot stress enough the importance for ministry of this sense of belonging to the world. There is a capacity to be moved to pity and a quality of showing kindness, exemplified in the story of the Good Samaritan, that can only come from a genuine identification with the world and its suffering people. This identity is called forth in us when we feel that we are one with the human race, not when we set ourselves apart from, or above others.

Fenhagen sees the task of the church today as engaging the world at every level with the claims and values of the gospel. At the heart of this understanding is something he calls a "holy worldliness"—a commitment to participate in the struggle of the world as one who knows the Lord. "Holy worldliness is life-affirming rather than pleasure-denying. It calls people to faith, not out of guilt or fear, but out of a vision of God that *evokes* response rather than commands it."[26] This can be done effectively only from within the community of the world.

Conclusion

The recovery of the broader ministry of baptism involves a growing understanding and acceptance of the many gifts and the diverse circumstances in which we live. We continue to reflect seriously on ways to make church ministry an effective and flourishing enterprise. We also need to acknowledge and take responsibility for the ministry in the marketplace. As we have shown, this ministry takes place in classrooms and boardrooms, on assembly lines and picket lines, in homes and at the office. These ministries are not different in nature, since all ministry flows from baptism and from the identity and intention of all believers.

The needs of our world require this broader view of ministry. The integrity of our faith and the dignity of each person invite it, and the power of the one Spirit allows it to flourish. Paul, spokesperson for the goodness of the variety of gifts says to the Corinthians:

> I am always thanking God for you. I thank God for the
> grace given to you in Christ Jesus. I thank God for all the

enrichment that has come to you in Christ. You possess full knowledge and you can give full expression to it, because in you the evidence for the truth of Christ has found confirmation. There is indeed no single gift you lack...It is the very God who called you to share in the life of God's son Jesus Christ our Lord; and God keeps faith (1 Cor 1:4–7, 9).

There is no gift we lack. Confidence in this promise and the joy that follows upon it must be the hallmarks of all ministry. What if ministry were to become the commission and the glory of all the baptized to all the world?[27]

NOTES

1. Some would respond by calling the daily work of Christians, "witness," leaving the term "ministry" to refer to official, public ministry.

2. The books I have surveyed include George Tavard's *The Pilgrim Church*, (1967); *A Theology for Ministry* (1983); Henri Nouwen's *Creative Ministry* (1971); Urban Holmes' *The Future Shape of Ministry* (1971), *Ministry and the Imagination* (1976) and in 1982, *Spirituality for Ministry;* Bernard Cooke's *Ministry to Word and Sacraments* (1976); David N. Power's *Gifts That Differ: Lay Ministries Established and Unestablished* (1980); Edward Schillebeeck's *Ministry: Leadership in the Community of Jesus Christ* (1981); and in 1985, *The Church with a Human Face: A New and Expanded Theology of Ministry;* Thomas O'Meara's *Theology of Ministry* (1983); John Macquarrie's *Theology, Church & Ministry* (1986); and Paul Bernier, *Ministry in the Church* (Mystic, CT: Twenty-Third Publications, 1992).

3. Urban Holmes, *The Future Shape of Ministry* (New York: The Seabury Press, 1971), p. 167.

4. See Edward Schillebeeckx, *Ministry* (New York: Crossroad, 1981), especially Chapter V, "A Brief Hermeneutical Intermezzo", pp. 100–104.

5. For a summary of many of these dialogues, see Bernard Cooke, *Ministry to Word and Sacraments,* (Philadelphia: Fortress, 1967), pp. 2–8.

6. Cooke, *Ministry,* p. 12. Cooke refers to documents on the priesthood produced at the last session of Vatican II: *Christus Dominus,*

Presbyterorum ordinis, and *Optatum totius,* and the ensuing commentaries. See S. Ryan, "The Hierarchical Structure of the Church," in *Vatican II: the Constitution on the Church,* ed. K. McNamara (London, 1968), pp. 163-234.

7. Hans Küng, *The Church* (London: Burns & Oates, 1968).

8. *The Church with a Human Face,* pp. 4–12.

9. Robert Kinast, "A Consultation with U.S. Lay People," *Origins* 16 (April 2, 1987): 733.

10. See *Gaudium et Spes* and *Lumen Gentium.* Also Paul VI, *Evangelii nuntiandi,* 1975. English translation: *On Evangelization in the Modern World* (Washington, D.C.: USCC, 1976).

11. See Rembert G. Weakland, "The Church in Worldly Affairs: Tensions Between Laity and Clergy," *America* (Oct. 18, 1986): 201–202.

12 Nouwen, *Creative Ministry,* p. xxi.

13. *Gifts That Differ,* p. 54.

14. Walter Brueggemann, "Why Prophets Won't Leave Well Enough Alone," *U.S. Catholic* 58 (January 1993): 9.

15. *Ministry to Word and Sacrament,* p. 190.

16. *Ministry and Solitude,* p. 18.

17. Ibid., p. 14. Thomas O'Meara underlines this same point: "The church is ministerial. Ministry is not a rare vocation or a privileged office but belongs to the nature of the new covenant. As with its universal source, baptism, ministry exists in the churches as an aspect of every Christian's life."*Theology of Ministry,* p. 209.

18. *Theology of Ministry,* p. 137.

19. *Ministry to Word,* p. 191.

20. Brueggemann, "Why Prophets...," p. 12.

21. Urban Holmes, *The Future Shape,* p. 113.

22. Cooke, *Ministry to Word,* p. vii.

23. Some examples include John Macquarrie, *Theology,* p. 157 and George Tavard, *A Theology for Ministry,* p. 97.

24. See Robert Bellah, et al. *Habits of the Heart: Individualism and Commitment in American Life* (Berkeley: University of California Press, 1985).

25. See Robert Farrar Capon, *An Offering of Uncles: The Priesthood of Adam and the Shape of the World* (New York: Crossroad, 1982).

26. *Ministry and Solitude,* p. 89.

27. O'Meara, *Theology of Ministry,* p. 3.

8

Sexuality: Meeting God in Human Love

In a book review in *Commonweal*, Eugene Kennedy states: "In no area is the humanity of the Catholic church—or its kinship with all other earthly institutions—more evident than in its attitudes toward sexuality, which are warped by ambiguity as thick and tingling as the air after a lightning storm."[1] This ambiguity has had unfortunate ramifications. It has taken the church until the mid-twentieth century to begin to teach that the sexual activity of married people, taken simply by itself, can express well their love. Only recently have Christian theologians begun to speak of the active giving and receiving of pleasure as not sinful.

But one rarely hears of the nobility of erotic love or of its ability to express aptly the personal love of the spouses and be the medium of their union. Leslie Dewart calls attention to the demeaning ways in which we continue to regard sexuality. It is not noble. It has not been a central element in the spiritual journey. He says:

> We do not ordinarily experience vividly, or with awe, God's wisdom in having created us male and female—along with all the personal sexuality of the individual which the generic bi-sexuality of the person implies. We are not often *glad*, precisely as Christians and in virtue of our faith, that sexuality exists. At best, we refrain from contempt.[2]

In light of such attitudes it seems odd indeed, that the church, and especially its mystics, have used the imagery of erotic love to describe the heights of union with God. It is not difficult to understand why persons experiencing extraordinary spiritual intimacy with God should turn to the human experience of sexual love to describe it. What we realize now is that authentic human erotic acts participate in the love of God and are a unitive force in the couple's love. In other words, they can become an integral part of our spiritual lives. I suggest that such a perspective is not only desirable but a necessary component of a thriving spiritual life.

Is the experience of a truly sanctified sexual life possible for us? Christian Catholic attitudes toward sexuality and the body have been so deeply problematic for so long, that one almost despairs of the possibility of shedding new light on the situation. But hope is rekindled when one surveys recent work in the area of sexuality and spirituality.[3] Historical studies on the origins and history of Christian attitudes toward the body and sexuality have been invaluable in furthering our understanding of those attitudes in their own time. These discoveries, in turn, mitigate the modern tendency to condemn the past *in toto* on this issue.[4] Reappraisals of the meaning of sexuality in the spiritual life are legion, pointing to the pressing need to address this issue in new and creative ways.[5] In the literature on Christian attitudes toward sexuality, the term "paradigm shift" occurs like a refrain. The challenge before us is to negotiate around a complex and entrenched tradition, in order to discern what should be left behind and what elements might be brought forward as we reflect on the spirituality of everyday life.

Past negative attitudes run deep and remain alive and well in the unconscious and conscious lives of ordinary people. In other areas of our lives, such as the economy, the military, and nuclear proliferation, the Roman Catholic bishops have attended more rigorously to the changing social context and have adjusted their positions in light of the wider sociocultural environment. But in the arena of sexuality, the emphasis remains on unchanging, "natural" and immutable elements with little or no regard for evolving scientific and social attitudes.[6]

However, theologians from a variety of perspectives continue to make contributions toward a contemporary understanding and practice of sexuality and its relationship to the spiritual life.[7] There are many reasons for this. The seeming omnipresence of sexuality in media and advertising demands examination and reflective assessment. And in addition to the foundational concerns discussed in Part I, the disciplines of psychology and biomedical science push on in their analysis of sexuality. Likewise, we have noted that the growing ecological crisis has forced us to reexamine our attitudes toward matter in general, and the body in particular. A spirituality that compartmentalizes the human person, eliminates the body from consideration, or worse, denigrates it, is no longer viable.

Our focus is the spirituality of everyday life. How are we to understand the role of the body and sexuality, as we experience them concretely each day, in terms of the journey toward God? My thesis is simple: There is something amiss if one's sexuality is not a primary locus of the revelation of God. As relational, sexuality is replete with potential elements for the spiritual life—self-knowledge; self-gift; love; kindness; intimacy; touch; kiss; embrace; nakedness; trust; vulnerability; pleasure; union; ecstasy; sense of the transcendent; play; self-denial; creativity; companionship; forgiveness. In this chapter I examine the meaning of sexuality; consider how selected aspects of the spiritual tradition might impinge positively on our understanding of sexuality and the spiritual life; and suggest elements for a contemporary understanding of sexuality and life in the Spirit.

I. THE MEANING OF SEXUALITY

A broad definition of sexuality might go something like this: human sexuality is that way of being in, and relating to, the world as a male or female person.[8] To be a sexual person means being sexually differentiated and relational. Sexual existence is corporeal, spiritual and social. It can be viewed from physical, social, psychological, personal or spiritual perspectives, but whatever we do, feel, think, or say, we do as sexual beings. We can talk about the affective dimension of sexuality (caring, friendship, tendernesss in our relationships) or the genital dimension—distinguishing, of course, in order to unite. We can propose ways to enhance our sexual existence as contributing to the fullness of life, as well as warn against abuses.

A 1977 document from the Sacred Congregation for the Doctrine of the Faith, *Persona Humana: Declaration on Sexual Ethics* (D.C.: USCC) says:

> It is from sex that the human person receives the characteristics which, on the biological basis, the psychological and spiritual levels, make that person a man or woman and thereby largely condition his or her progress towards maturity and insertion into society (n. 1, p. 3).

And one might add, "toward holiness." Human sexuality is a fundamental modality by which we relate to ourselves, to other persons, to the universe and to God. In order to gain a fuller appreciation of the role of sexuality in spirituality, we need to find language and images that will adequately express our experience as women and men.

In modern culture, sexuality is often trivialized. But unlike the more mundane and routine operations of daily life, sexuality is a powerful, driving force. It belongs to the world of love and sin and grace and death, not to the realm of getting dressed or driving a car. The intrinsic power of sexuality should caution against a glib, off-hand, careless treatment. It merits awe, reverence, respect. On the other hand, fear of its power has led to irrational apprehensions and brutal suppression, alienating us from this integral and sacred dimension of human existence.

In the last analysis, from a faith perspective, sexuality is a marvelous gift, a central element in a good creation made by a generous and loving God. God's image is reflected in the totality of our being. We remind ourselves that the meaning of human sexuality and its relationship to our daily spiritual lives comes from us, individually and as a community, and does not drop down from heaven. Meaning is best determined by the collaboration of many—the community of believers, the medical community, scientists, counsellors, theologians, and religious leaders. The questions of *who* has given meaning to sexuality and *when* that meaning was given are important to keep before us. Now let us examine several aspects of the tradition as it has approached the topic of sexuality.

II. SEXUALITY AND THE TRADITION

The gospels themselves say little about the topic and there is certainly no disparagement of sexuality on the part of Jesus. It simply does not play an important part in the community's narratives about him. The early Christian community came to understand sexuality over against pagan practices, such as temple prostitution, that were thought to be contrary to Christianity. Thus, teaching on sexuality emerged out of a reaction to practices beyond and, at times, within the fold.

Further, the society in which Christianity was inserted was often puzzled and scandalized by what they heard about Christian practices. Some of these practices, in which Christians strove to overcome the distinctions between female and male (Gal 3.28), involved women and men in relationships that were foreign to accepted social norms. In response to the scandal taken by the larger society, Christians adopted very strict attitudes toward sexuality in order to diffuse charges of promiscuity and immorality.

We have noted the dual roots of Christianity in the Hebrew and Greek worlds. In some ways the Hebrew concept of the human person was more holistic than that of the Greeks, but there is also a great deal of attention paid in the Hebrew scriptures to the ritual impurity that resulted from sexual activity. And several strains of Greek philosophy held that matter was evil in itself. As a result, the body was seen as evil, and in order to be holy, one had to escape from it. Epicurus, a Stoic philosopher, wrote that sexual intercourse never did a man good, and he was lucky if it did not harm him!

This polarity is already present in the New Testament. At least two of the reasons Paul advocates celibacy are that it was his own preferred lifestyle and, second, it seemed reasonable to advocate celibacy at a time when the community was waiting for the imminent end of the world. It did not make sense to marry, when tomorrow the whole community might be entering into eternity where there would be no marriage.

We also struggle with a consistent misunderstanding of the term "flesh" in Paul's letters.[9] For Paul, human action and attitudes fell into two categories—they either brought you closer to

God, and were called "spirit," or they moved you away from God and were labelled "flesh." Thus it would be possible to have a prayer life that was "flesh" and a sex life that was "spirit." Paul was not condemning embodiment. "Flesh" meant that which was weak, corruptible, not of God. It did not refer primarily to our bodies considered as material substances. He had no intention of contrasting the material body of the human person with the spiritual component of the soul. Later, Neoplatonic dualistic understandings led to a false ascetical ideal in which the body was despised, and holiness became synonymous with the rejection of physical pleasure, primarily the pleasures of sex and eating. The struggle to overcome dualistic attitudes continues into our own day.

The history of the early church is, in part, a struggle to synthesize these two quite different strains with the astounding fact of incarnation, that is, a God who assumed a body out of love for the human race. Our lack of success is visible in the inconsistency in Christianity between the negative attitude toward sexuality and the primacy given to the unique value of love. The tradition is replete with statements that clash in modern consciousness—on the one hand a rhetoric of disparagement of the body, and on the other, theological descriptions of the permanent integrity of body and soul, based on the incarnation.[10] In many ways, the early church retreated from the implications of the incarnation.[11] Happily we are becoming more aware of, and sensitive to, the possibilities of a truly incarnational spirituality.

The subsequent history of Christian attitudes toward sexuality is *complex* and *diverse*. No single understanding of sexuality can lay claim to exclusive authenticity in the tradition. Teaching on sexuality has varied from one era to another and from writer to writer within each period.

One can also say with confidence that sexuality has not been trivialized in the Christian tradition. It was always treated with great seriousness. While this is a positive development in the tradition, there is also a negative side. In fact, it is puzzling that sexuality took on tones of such enormous importance and weight. At times, one thinks we might have been better off if sexuality had been seen in a wider perspective and treated with a certain amount of benign neglect. We can be instructed by the medieval poet, Dante Alighieri (d. 1321), who wisely places sexual sins in the second circle of hell, far removed from the most serious sins at the bottom.[12]

A sexual ethic of abstinence pervaded the views of the early church fathers. While on many fronts the church defended the body and sexuality against hostile social attitudes, it was rarely concerned about how marriage and sexuality might be central elements on the road to holiness.

The charism of virginity became absolutized, institutionalized, mandated by law. Without detracting from the value of the authentic charism of virginity, one cannot but be saddened at the price paid by sexuality and marriage.[13]

During the early Middle Ages—the sixth to tenth centuries—a body of literature arose called "the penitentials," in which a great deal of attention was paid to sexual sin and to rules governing sexual activity.[14] Married couples were permitted to have intercourse only a few times a year. Marital sex was forbidden on fast days, on feast days, before communion, and after receiving the sacrament, during Lent, Advent, and Whitsuntide, on certain days of each week, and during menstruation, pregnancy, and lactation! To this literature, we owe the pithy medieval statement—"Thank God it's Monday"—the only day on which sex was allowed![15]

But in spite of these damaging attitudes, I suggest that the tradition is also a potentially fruitful resource, provided that we transpose past ideas into a new key that will harmonize with contemporary perceptions and needs.

Positive Elements in the Tradition

We can identify several positive strains in the tradition. Many early Christian writers were men who had married, raised Christian families and made significant contributions to the societies in which they lived before turning to the celibate lifestyle and church leadership. One also thinks of the women and men who collaborated in any number of ways in carrying out their Christian vocation—Jerome and Melania; Basil, Gregory and their sister, Macrina; Francis and Clare; Eloise and

Abelard; Teresa of Avila and Gracian; Jane de Chantal and Francis de Sales; Louise de Marillac and Vincent de Paul. These well-known figures reveal that some of the energy of their efforts to carry out the mission of Jesus was sparked by their relationships with someone of the opposite sex.

We also have texts that examine the human experience of friendship with its pleasures and rewards—texts that place friendship on the wider canvas of the Christian life and of one's relationship with God. One is struck by the erotic imagery used by medieval female and male mystics alike.[16] The imagery of sexual love, often taken from the Song of Songs, seemed to be a particularly apt way to describe the heights of mystical union. In this age of mysticism, courtly love and romance, the imagery of the Song of Songs captured the imagination of both Christians and Jews. This mystical literature can be an important resource in our attempt to create a contemporary theology of sexuality.[17]

One cannot but note the clash between the use of this imagery and the accompanying fear and denigration of actual physical love in its fleshly reality.[18] We need to appropriate this imagery in a new key as *connected* to our actual bodily, sexual existence. We have noted that the primary religious mandate for the laity was not mystical marriage but obedience to the ten commandments. Only virginal religious and clergy were expected to enter into the heights of mystical union. Is it possible to make use of this tradition in our present circumstances? We offer two specific examples.

Bodily Knowing

In a recent article entitled, "A Medieval Lesson on Bodily Knowing: Women's Experience and Men's Thought," J. Giles Milhaven of Brown University addresses the question of how persons came to know in the Middle Ages and today.[19] He notes that the tradition has rarely regarded bodies and feelings as primary loci for God's presence. I believe that we continue to be deadened in significant ways to this truth, making it difficult for us to discover God present in these arenas of human experience.

Milhaven turns to art in order to relate the point of bodily knowing to our own experience. Traditional Christian philosophy understood the unitive dynamic of the devout person viewing the *Pietà*, for example, as immaterial, non-physical. One knew Mary by bodiless intellect and loved her and felt with her by means of a bodiless will.[20] The viewer's physical experience of the sculpture is necessary only as a context for the viewer to unite with Mary spiritually. But Milhaven raises a challenging question:

> This traditional theory is contradicted by the impact of the *Pietà* on many devout believers...The direct conscious union of the devout person with the mourning mother is inextricably both physical and personal...The physical is the personal. The personal is the physical.

If devout persons were to abstract from their bodily aching with the grief-struck Mary, there would be little of moment left of that first, immediate experience of Mary.

The Western tradition remains true to its Greek roots inasmuch as it gives short shrift to bodily knowing. This knowing remained the lowest kind of human knowing, unable to represent anything intrinsically valuable. Bodily knowing is knowledge of the particular, and only universal knowledge was considered true knowledge. Bodily knowing also involves touch, the sense considered to be the lowest of senses because it was least like reason. Further, the kinds of touch commonly reported in the mystical accounts of medieval women were considered the least valuable—satisfaction of hunger or sex appetite, hugging, weariness. "The women seek and enjoy eating and drinking Christ, caressing and nursing Christ, making love and playing with Christ, embracing the suffering or dead Christ."[21]

Milhaven then moves his argument into even more accessible territory—the family. He suggests that some of the greatest mutual awareness in families takes place through touch. Is it not at times the most precious knowledge of each other that we have? And does it not have the potential to put us in touch with God? Touch is central not only to eating and drinking together, nursing, playing with the children and having sex, but also to supporting children taking their first steps, clothing them, embracing the bereaved, holding the hand of the sick, sleeping together, the adult hug of reunion after long separation. One can move quite easily from family to extended family, to friends and lovers of all stripes.

Bodily knowing also produces personal and physical identification.[22] The medieval women who keep vigil with Christ in his passion and death become one with him suffering. They weep with Mary sorrowing. They laugh with the joy of the child in their arms. This kind of bodily knowing is available to us in our lives, but may be ignored, as it was by most medieval theologians, because of their fear or of narrow theological and spiritual categories.

Medieval theologians were unable to appreciate the wisdom coming from "the ordinary love and pleasure of living together in a family, of eating day after day at the same table, as well as of making love."[23] Traditional Christian thinkers did not acknowledge that if they used a reality of this world to image something beyond this world, the worldly reality was similar to the heavenly reality to which it pointed and in which it participated. Have we been so preoccupied with the imperfections of human sexuality that we have missed its godly character altogether?

Perhaps the medieval women were right. Not only by reason, but also in and through their bodies do human beings know much that is intrinsically precious in human life. In and through their bodies they came to know and to love the Lord.[24] We have known for a long time that one can know through reason. Perhaps the time has come for us to add bodily knowing to our repertoire.

The Image of the Kiss in the Tradition

Another theme from the medieval mystical traditon—the image of the kiss—can be critically reappropriated and *connected* with our experiences of human love. For many persons, the kiss is a frequent daily occurrence. There are routine social kisses among friends and colleagues. There are joyful, appreciative kisses that parents plant on children. There are perfunctory "Kiss and Ride" kisses of spouses going off to work. There are tender, healing kisses; intense, passionate kisses; and lives with no kisses at all. How often do we connect all these kisses with our spiritual lives?

The excerpts I have chosen are from Bernard of Clairvaux's *Sermons on the Song of Songs.* This text, a series of conferences in which Bernard interprets the beginning verses of the Song, is said to be a synthesis of the whole of his spiritual teaching.[25] It is a prime example of much medieval mystical literature that employs the Song to speak of the spiritual life in terms of the image of lovers. We note again the medieval emphasis on the purely spiritual nature of this love. Such texts are addressed to those monastics advanced in the spiritual life—those who realize that the love talk in the Song does not refer in any way to bodily, physical love. But we may well ask what is implied in this use of the image of the kiss?

Given the Neoplatonic worldview that Bernard inherited, he expresses a surprisingly high regard for the body. He acknowledges that souls need bodies because they mediate a kind of knowledge by which one is elevated toward the contemplation of truths essential to happiness.[26] Created spirits need bodies in order to assist and be assisted by others.[27] And because no created spirit can of itself act directly on our minds, we need the mediation of a bodily instrument to make contact with our minds in order to acquire knowledge and virtue.[28]

Bernard develops at some length the image of the kiss found in the first verse of the Song:

> I will sing the song of all songs to Solomon that he may smother me with kisses.

The level of intimacy between the soul and God intensifies as the soul moves from the kiss of the feet to the kiss of the hands to the kiss of the mouth. So too, in human lovemaking, the kiss is often a prelude to a more intense and intimate encounter. The passages that suggest such an intimate encounter are numerous. For instance, in sermon eight, Bernard compares the spiritual union of the mystic with God to the bodily union of a married couple. He says:

For if marriage according to the flesh constitutes two in one body, why should not a spiritual union be even more efficacious in joining two in one spirit?[29]

In a second passage, Bernard underlines the primacy of desire over reason. The bride speaks:

"I cannot rest," she said, "unless he kisses me with the kiss of his mouth...There is no question of ingratitude on my part, it is simply that I am in love. The favors I have received are far above what I deserve, but they are less than what I long for. It is desire that drives me on, not reason. Please do not accuse me of presumption if I yield to this impulse of love.[30]

Often this literature employs talk about inebriation to communicate the sense of ecstasy or loss of control that accompanies a mystical encounter. Bernard suggests that one would have to be drunk not only to open oneself to, but to seek, such an intimate union with God. God is the one at whose glance the earth trembles, and yet the bride demands a kiss. He says:

Can she possibly be drunk? Absolutely drunk! And the reason? It seems most probable that when she uttered those passionate words she had just come out from the cellar of wine; afterwards she boasts of having been there.[31]

Bernard then quotes David from the Psalms: "They shall be inebriated with the plenty of your house; and you will make them drink of the torrent of your pleasure."[32]

In a final citation, Bernard adds the image of conception to that of the kiss:

While the bride is conversing about the Bridegroom, he, as I have said, suddenly appears, yields to her desire by giving her a kiss...The filling up of her breasts is a proof of this. For so great is the potency of that holy kiss, that no sooner has the bride received it than she conceives and her breasts grow rounded with the fruitfulness of conception, bearing witness, as it were, with this milky abundance.[33]

Why cannot this portrayal of an intimate spiritual love of God inspire our relationships with a human beloved and connect them with the spiritual life? Bernard counsels his listeners to learn a love that is tender, wise, strong. Love with tenderness, wisdom and strength, he admonishes his brothers, so as not to grow weary and turn away from the love of the Lord.[34]

Love relationships that include physical intimacy are prime candidates for this kind of deferent, reverential, tender commitment. And conversely, our experience of the giftedness of such love with another human being can provide a touchstone for the lifelong journey toward ever greater intimacy with God. For too long, the church and its theologians have ignored the wisdom that comes from authentic sexual love and pleasure.

In honoring our bodies and our sexuality, we need to remember that it is through the body with its senses that we encounter each other—sight, touch, smell, sound. And we might reflect on Jesus of Nazareth as an eminent example of one who touched and was touched by others.

Our relationships with each other as sexual beings have everything to do with God and with life in the Spirit. The gift of loving human relationships is a primary indicator of who God is—the ultimate lover. In a paradigmatic way, the total love between persons that includes the physical, intellectual and spiritual dimensions of existence points to the love of God for us. Instead of regarding sexual encounter as something shady or embarrassing, we are invited today to see sexuality as integral to growth in the Spirit, to growth in self-transcending love. Scripture tells us that loving gestures toward others are considered gestures toward God (Mt 25). To offer and receive love in the range and fullness of its expression is one important aspect of the royal road to holiness.

III. TWO THEOLOGICAL CONSIDERATIONS

Some members of the Christian community are beginning to rediscover joy in all the aspects that make us human and to connect these daily experiences with our spiritual well-being. We need now to inquire about how we think theologically about this connection. Let us examine two theological concepts that ground the connection between sexuality and life in the Spirit: the belief that we are made in the image of God; and the experience of sexual union as a sacrament of the unity of the world.

Image of God

More and more, theologians are emphasizing the communal rather than the individual aspects of faith and religious experience.[35] The intimate relationships and communication within the Trinity are often pointed to as a model for the kind of total, intimate human relationship of which we have been speaking. Both in our individuality and in all of our daily human encounters, we are called to be and to become the image of God, credible symbols of trinitarian love.[36]

Trinitarian theology also holds that the total surrender and unity of each person does not destroy but rather fulfills the uniqueness of each. So, too, two persons who give themselves fully to each other do not lose themselves, but rather find themselves in the growing fullness of their existence. Such authentic love is appealing to others. As the open, tender and perfect love within God draws us toward God,[37] so this kind of love in the human community draws others by its alluring example.

> Truly intimate couples bring people into the Church by witnessing to the inner life of God. For membership in the Church is a life, a life of not just imitating but participating in the very life of God. The Church is, then, really a community of intimates. Even though no one ever observes them in the act of making love, their transfiguration has its effects on all who know them. They become credible symbols. Other people see that they have something, something that makes life deeply joyous and satisfying.[38]

The Trinity symbolizes not only the mutual love among persons, but also the fruit of that love. As we have seen, the Holy Spirit is the bond, the nexus, the fruit of the love between the Mother/Father and the Son. An intimate, free and loving surrender of one person to another does not turn inward, imploding on itself. Divine love is reflected in the human community as our love moves out beyond itself—from the conception of another human being to an embrace that encompasses the entire cosmos. While witnessing to the intimacy of God is the mandate of all the baptized, married persons incarnate trinitarian love in a truly distinctive way.

Bodiliness is also a leitmotif in the Christian tradition. The Christian God is one who assumed a physical body. We use bodily language and imagery to speak of the church. We refer to ourselves as the "body of Christ" and as the "mystical body." The names of churches and feast days and religious orders abound with body imagery—Corpus Christi, Heart of Mary, Sacred Heart, Immaculate Conception, Precious Blood. There is no longer any reason for us to separate such language and imagery from our physical, bodily existence. In fact, the respect and reverence we experience with regard to our bodiliness (created by God and sanctified by the incarnation) and to our relationships with others, grounds and gives depth of meaning to our religious language about bodiliness.

The church as the body of Christ reminds us of the wondrous variety exhibited in the parts of the body; of the mutual interdependence and connectedness of each part; of the nurture and sustenance of eating and drinking the body and blood of Christ; of the unity for which we strive in the midst of the many diverse gifts among us; of mutual service and risk-taking as we strive to lay down our lives for each other. How lamentable it is when we fail to understand these profound truths in terms of everyday existence—colleagues at work, good friends celebrating and mourning, family members in the home, spouses in the bedroom, persons suffering illness and oppression, persons across the globe.

To speak of God's love for the world, we use images of shepherd, loving parent, friend, king/queen, healer. In addition to these metaphors, we need to explore the powerful image of God as passionate lover and spouse.[39] This image of God comes forth in part from our experience of the sacredness of being passionate lovers. In turn, the biblical image of God as passionate lover, reinforces our own loving as we strive to be imitators of God. Perhaps as we become more comfortable with our sexual selves,[40] we will see more clearly the Yahweh who is the Spouse of Israel, the God who is the beloved of each person and of the church.[41] Allowing oneself to enter into a nuptial relationship with another human being and with God can only be mutually enhancing. Our human loves are irrevocably tied up with God and God's loves are irrevocably tied up with us.

Sexuality as Sacrament

Theologians also examine intimate human love in terms of its sacramentality.[42] Philip Sherrard begins his book, *Christianity and Eros* as follows: "The idea of the sacramental potentiality of sexual love is one of the most creative and ennobling ideas in which the European imagination has shared."[43] Joan Timmerman defines sacramentality as "the capacity of the world to reveal, and the person to apprehend, the mysterious presence of God."[44] Sacramental reality is any reality that makes us aware of God's presence, that puts us in touch with the awesome mystery that is God. As we have proposed throughout this discussion, the realities that are a sacrament of God in a primordial sense, are the daily activities of living, loving, and working.

The recovery of the sacramental nature of sexuality demands the dismantling of the wall set up between divine love and human sexual love.[45] We need to endow human sexuality with an authentic sacramentality; that is, human sexual activity, as a sacrament of union with God, must be seen as capable of being transformed and of revealing God through the deepening mutual sense of each other's being. The fullness of a relationship between two persons becomes a primary vehicle for personal holiness and union with God. Such sacramentality is based on the theological conviction that sexual relationships have their very foundation in the divine reality. In moving toward God, one must also move toward, not away from, one's sexual existence.

Second, we can begin to see our bodies and sexual activity as connected with the sacramentality of all of nature. Nature has always been a common entrée into the reality of God. Early in life, one is often first aware of the beauty and magnitude of God in nature—in the depths of the ocean, in the shape of a flower petal or in the profound hues of a sunset. The wonder and reverence that the natural world calls forth can be transferred to our own bodiliness. In a distinctive way, our bodies connect us with the rest of material creation. Perhaps, too, there are connections between disregard for our own bodies and the consistent destruction of the universe.

In addition to being a sacrament of the unity of two persons and of the unity between persons and God, sexuality can function as a sacrament of the unity of the world.[46] Sexuality is an impulse to relationship. The very meaning of sexuality emerges out of the community into which one is born, and the experience of authentic love between two persons does not stop with the individuals involved but redounds to the larger community. As growth in spirituality gradually widens one's horizons of love to include all peoples and things, it is also appropriate to understand the sexual relationship as a symbol that points to, and brings about, the unity of the world.

Travel and instant satellite communications make us aware that we live in a global village. No one doubts that we are going to have to figure out how to live in peace with those on the entire planet and indeed, with the ecosystem itself. We can be greatly assisted in this task if we are able to connect the loving struggles of our sexual relationships with this broader canvas.

Sexual love can be not only an experience of mystery and grace, but a conduit extending the care between two persons to care for the world. Conversely, we need to connect the expression of loving care and personal dignity in our world with our sexual activity. It would be a failure for the church, theologians, and individual Christians to continue to view sexuality in the narrow terms of two persons and their immediate family. What happens in the bedroom and in the daily round of activities ripples outward toward the world and either builds up or tears down attempts to bring about a just world which all can call home.

Falling in love allows the giftedness of the transcendent to break into one's consciousness. The ecstasy of sexual attraction and consummation is the grace of vocation, the "beginning of a call to sacramental sexuality."[47]

Our sexuality is a sacrament of God, a sacred locus where we discover ourselves, other persons and all of creation in God. It is a sacrament which can engage our creativity, renew our commitment, and fire our courage to work together to mediate the kingdom of God in history; that is, to work toward a just and peaceful world.

Conclusion

We can learn to celebrate the goodness of our sexuality and to lament abuses in the context of our spirituality. We can grow to appreciate the enormous variety of sexual expression as myriad ways to reflect and give praise to God in much the same way as we regard variety in other aspects of life—personalities, species, colors, foods, clothing.[48] We may also begin to see the negation of one's bodiliness and sexuality as a diminishment of one's humanity and therefore as sinful. To refuse to be vulnerable; to refuse to open oneself to another; to abuse or manipulate or treat another carelessly; to cling and be possessive—all are steps away from God. On the other hand, authentic sexual experience can be a major means to overcome egoism, to discover God, and to grow in self-transcending love. It is a part of human experience that should be at the center of one's life in the Spirit.

Finally, in a more overtly religious vein, we are invited to reflect prayerfully on the biblical tradition—the Genesis story of creation; the Song of Songs; the role of Mary and Joseph; the humanity of Jesus; the "touching" stories in the gospel; the marriage feast at Cana, the importance given to marriage and family in Jesus' Jewish community.

It is obvious that the answer to the question of whether we are able to experience a sacralized sexuality is affirmative. We are continually reminded that all is grace. We have been made in our totality by a generous and loving God and in God's image.

> The final infolding of mutual love, that alone in which the fully sacramental union between man and woman is

achieved, is not an acquisition but a benediction. It is conferred by the Creator on two creatures, man and woman, who have run the course of their love through whatever it may have led them and have entered, transfigured at last, the holy ground of their being.[49]

NOTES

1. Eugene Kennedy, "Homosexual Priests and Nuns: Two Assessments" *Commonweal* 117 (1990): 56-57.

2. Leslie Dewart, "*Casti Connubii* and the Development of Dogma," in Thomas D. Roberts, *Contraception and Holiness: The Catholic Predicament* (New York: Herder and Herder, 1964), pp. 205–06.

3. Two early works are Charles Davis' *Body as Spirit: The Nature of Religious Feeling* (New York: Seabury, 1976); and Philip Sherrard's *Christianity and Eros: Essays on the Theme of Sexual Love* (London: SPCK, 1976).

4. See Peter Brown, *The Body and Society: Men, Women and Sexual Renunciation in Early Christianity* (New York: Columbia University Press, 1988); Pierre J. Payer, *Sex and the Penitentials* (Toronto: University of Toronto Press, 1986); Jean Leclercq, *Monks on Marriage: A Twelfth-Century View* (New York: Seabury, 1982) and *Monks and Love in Twelfth-Century France* (Oxford: Clarendon Press, 1979); Kari Elisabeth Borreson, *Subordination and Equivalence: The Nature and Role of Woman in Augustine and Thomas Aquinas* (Washington, D.C.:University Press of America, 1981); Margaret Miles, *Practicing Christianity: Critical Perspectives for an Embodied Spirituality* (New York: Crossroad, 1988).

5. See Joan Timmerman, *The Mardi Gras Syndrome: Rethinking Christian Sexuality* (New York: Crossroad, 1985) and *Sexuality and Spiritual Growth* (New York: Crossroad, 1992); James B. Nelson, *Embodiment* (Minneapolis: Augsburg, 1978); John Moore, *Sexuality and Spirituality: The Interplay of Masculine and Feminine in Human Development* (San Francisco: Harper & Row, 1980), a psychological, sociobiological approach; Dorothy Soelle, with Shirley A Cloyes, *To Work and To Love* (Philadelphia: Fortress, 1984); Gallagher, C., Maloney, Rousseau, Wilczak, *Embodied in Love: Sacramental Spirituality and Sexual Intimacy* (New York: Crossroad, 1985); Sylvia Chavez-Garcia and Daniel A. Helminiak, "Sexuality and Spirituality: Friends Not

Foes," *The Journal of Pastoral Care* 34(1985): 151–163; and Patricia Treece, *The Sanctified Body* (New York: Doubleday, 1989).

6. See Charles Curran, "Catholic Social and Sexual Teachings: A Methodological Comparison," *Theology Today* (January 1988): 425–440.

7. Moral theologians are perhaps the most prolific writers on the topic of sexuality. See review of six recent works (Lisa Sowle Cahill, Letha Dawson Scanzoni, Gallagher/Maloney/Rousseau/Wilczak, Beverly Wildung Harrison, James B. Nelson, and Andre Guindon) by Christine E. Gudorf and Robert W. Blaney in *Religious Studies Review* 14(April 1988): 125–131. All the books begin by pointing out that Christian attitudes toward and treatment of sexuality are in need of fundamental correction.

8. Gennaro Avvento, *Sexuality: A Christian View* (Mystic, CT: Twenty-Third Publications, 1982), p. 19. Recent studies on human sexuality sponsored by the United Church of Christ, the Catholic Theological Association of America, and the United Church of Canada distinguish between "sex"—genital sex—and "sexuality"—a more inclusive, holistic understanding of sexuality including the emotional, physical, cognitive, spiritual, personal and social dimensions of one's experience.

9. In a comment on Jerome's exegesis of Paul, Peter Brown states: "In his exegesis of the Apostle, he contributed more heavily than did any other contemporary Latin writer to the definitive sexualization of Paul's notion of *the flesh.*" *The Body and Society,* p. 376.

10. Ibid., p. 95.

11. Rowan Williams, *Christian Spirituality: A Theological History from the New Testament to Luther and John of the Cross* (Atlanta: John Knox Press, 1979), p. 21. See also Margaret Miles, *Practicing Christianity*, pp. 99, 156.

12. Dante Alighieri, *The Divine Comedy, Inferno,* Canto V.

13. See Peter Brown, "The Notion of Virginity in the Early Church." In *Christian Spirituality: Origins to the Twelfth Century.* Eds. B. McGinn and J. Meyendorf (New York: Crossroad, 1986), pp. 427–443; and John Bugge, "Virginitas: An Essay in the History of a Medieval Idea," *Archives internationale d'histoire des idées,* 17 (The Hague, 1975).

14. See *Sex and the Penitentials* by Pierre J. Payer (Toronto: University of Toronto Press, 1986).

15. See Joan Timmerman, *The Mardi-Gras Syndrome.*

16. In the twelfth century, most persons entering religious life were not children but mature adults many of whom had experienced courtship, marriage and family life before becoming monks or nuns.

See Jean Leclercq, *Monks and Love in Twelfth-Century France: Psycho-Historical Essays,* (London: Oxford University Press, 1979) and Caroline Walker Bynum, *Jesus as Mother* (Berkeley, CA: University of California Press, 1982), p. 142.

17. See E. Ann Matter, *The Voice of My Beloved: The Song of Songs in Western Medieval Christianity* (Philadelphia: University of Pennsylvania Press, 1990); and Marcia Falk The *Song of Songs* (San Francisco: HarperCollins, 1990).

18. Speaking of Hildegard of Bingen's (1098–1179) accounts of her mystical experience, Barbara Newman notes how the reader is jarred by her "bold, affirmative view of sexual symbolism and a largely negative view of sexual practice." In *Sister of Wisdom: St. Hildegard's Theology of the Feminine* (Berkeley, CA: University of California Press, 1987), p. 21.

19. J. Giles Milhaven, "A Medieval Lesson on Bodily Knowing: Women's Experience and Men's Thought." *Journal of the American Academy of Religion* 57 (1989):341–372. See also "The Church and Erotic Love in Marriage," *New Catholic World* 220 (1977):246–67.

20. Ibid., p. 354.

21. Ibid., p. 359.

22. Ibid., p. 365.

23. Ibid., p. 362.

24. Ibid., p. 368.

25. Bernard of Clairvaux, *On The Song of Songs* (Spencer, MA: Cistercian Publications, 1971), 4 vols. Vol 1, p. ix.

26. Ibid., Sermon 5.1.

27. Ibid., Sermon 5.6.

28. Ibid., Sermon 5.8.

29. Ibid., Sermon 8.9.

30. Ibid., Sermon 9.2.

31. Ibid., Sermon 7.3.

32. Psalm 35.9.

33. *On the Song of Songs,* Sermon 9.7.

34. Ibid., Sermon 20.4.

35. Historian Michel Foucault posits that desire for sexual pleasure is not a "natural" state that exists prior to society, but rather that the process of socialization within a particular culture creates a sexuality that serves social ends. This thesis connects sexuality with social values rather than primarily with those of the individual. *History of Sexuality,* (New York: Random House, 1978).

36. C. Gallagher, et al. *Embodied in Love,* p. 25. See also

Catherine M. LaCugna's *God For Us: The Trinity and Christian Life* (Harper San Francisco, 1991), pp. 243–317 and 404–408.

37. Julian of Norwich has written one of the most powerful accounts of the dynamic, intimate, joyful love among the persons of the Trinity. *Showings* (New York: Paulist Press, 1978).

38. C. Gallagher, et al., *Embodied Love*, p. 110.

39. See Rosemary Haughton, *The Passionate God* (New York: Paulist Press, 1981); and Sally McFague, *Models of God* (Philadelphia: Fortress Press, 1987).

40. It may seem odd to speak of being uncomfortable with sexuality in a society that seems to be obsessed with it. But I suggest that the church's failure to deal with sexuality in a reverent, forthright and open manner contributes both to our continuing discomfort and even in some measure, to sexual exploitation.

41. For concrete ways in which church structure might reflect nuptial love, see C. Gallagher, *Embodied in Love*, pp. 117–136.

42. See especially Joan Timmerman, *The Mardi Gras Syndrome;* C. Gallagher et al. *Embodied in Love;* Margaret Miles, *Practicing Christianity*, chapter 6: "The Word Made Flesh: Worship and Sacraments", pp. 105–113.

43. Philip Sherrard, *Christianity and Eros: Essays on the Theme of Sexual Love* (London: SPCK, 1976), p. 1.

44. The *Mardi Gras Syndrome*, p. ix.

45. One also needs to eliminate the rift between the church's affirmation of the sacramental dignity of marriage and its consistent denial of the inherent goodness of sexual activity.

46. See Joan Timmerman, *The Mardi Gras Syndrome*, pp. 57–61.

47. C. Gallagher, et al., *Embodied in Love*, p. 36.

48. Joan Timmerman, *The Mardi Gras Syndrome*, p. 16.

49. P. Sherrard, *Christianity and Eros*, p. 93.

9

Asceticism Revisited

"Asceticism" is the traditional term used to refer to the practice of self-denial as a religious discipline. It is a strong word—like "grace" and "sin" and "saint"—deserving to be reclaimed rather than rejected. Indeed, several theologians are grappling with how to recover and renew this age-old spiritual tradition.[1] One reason for this renewed interest in asceticism is the discomfort many Americans feel about our enormous wealth vis-à-vis so many other countries, and our accompanying penchant toward consumerism. We search to moderate our consuming ways. Some long for what seemed to be a more rigorous way of life in which character formation and discipline held a more prominent place than did consumption. But it is all too clear that returning to the Friday fast and giving up candy for Lent will not alone serve our present needs adequately.

Christian life would obviously be impoverished were traditional forms of asceticism eliminated. At its best, asceticism can be viewed as a way to the fullness of life, a way to ward off the death-dealing power of idolatry, of obsessive compulsions, of illusion and egoism. Physical asceticism, such as fasting, is often practiced as a way to protest against injustice or as a sign of solidarity with those who are oppressed and suffering. Ascetic practices can foster conversion, gather and focus energy, enhance service to the neighbor, and when reconnected with love, keep at bay the dangers of self-preoccupation and self-congratulation.

Theologians, pastors, and everyday Christians approach asceticism from a variety of perspectives—a beneficial phenomenon in itself. One popular approach is to begin with traditional activities, such as fasting and abstinence, and to recover their meaning within a contemporary, spiritual framework. While valid and often helpful, this route fails to take adequate account of the broader canvas of daily life. A second, more penetrating method aims to renew the way we have understood asceticism by taking everyday experience as its starting point.

In order to situate ourselves on the larger map of asceticism, I begin with some historical background, followed by one example of how the medieval tradition can serve as a positive resource in our present task. Then I develop this alternative viewpoint that places ordinary, everyday experience at the heart of asceticism.

I. HISTORICAL BACKGROUND

Nearly all religions have encouraged believers to engage in behavior that is characterized by some renunciation of the social and physical world. In the Greek world into which a nascent Christianity moved, *ascesis* referred to training, exercise or practice. At first, it referred to the achievement of bodily excellence—its perduring legacy being the Olympic Games. Later it was extended to the training of the mind in the acquisition of wisdom, and to training in virtue—disciplining and strengthening the will in order to turn away from all forms of self-indulgence, especially wine, food, sex.[2] In the Hebrew community, periodic fasting was a custom enjoined on all believers. The prophets repeatedly counseled the community in times of national crisis to fast, to repent, to alter habitual behavior, in order to wake up to some impending disaster.[3]

There was a particularly strong ascetic streak in the Christian community from the third to the fifth centuries A.D. The Alexandrians, Clement (d.c. 215) and Origen (d. 254), incorporated the idea of ascetic behavior into their theologies. Perhaps the name most frequently associated with asceticism is that of Antony (d. 356), the monk—immortalized in Athansius' famous biography—who retired to the desert to fight the demons, protesting the wedding of church and state after Constantine.[4]

This tradition continued through the age of the martyrs and into the Middle Ages, during which time we witness some extreme forms of ascetic behavior. Almost all medieval saints put a high priority on self-denial. One of the most well-known is Francis of Assisi (d. 1226) who treated his own "Brother Body" with great severity, requesting to die naked on the bare earth. Lay groups, called "penitents," were also popular in the Middle Ages, parading through the streets of Europe in sackcloth and ashes. In some religious orders, ascetic practices such as fasting, flagellations, and the use of chains and hair shirts continued in some form well into this century, especially in Europe.

In its more striking forms, Christian asceticism has been characterized by withdrawal from society, flight into the desert, open struggle with demonic forces, fasting, constant prayer, sleep deprivation, virginity, a strong sense of the end of the world, and self-inflicted mortification, often in imitation of hero-martyrs.[5]

As we saw in Part I, Greek dualism influenced the early Christians away from an incarnational theology and toward viewing the body as a major obstacle to holiness, in constant need of containment, suppression, control. This influence, in varying form and strength, has perdured down to the present. But since we no longer aspire to this dualistic view of body/soul, we have a hard time understanding why or how this kind of asceticism could be beneficial. It seems unhealthy at best and perhaps even harmful to full human development.

Given this heritage, we inquire whether the Christian spiritual tradition has anything positive to offer us in our quest for a renewed understanding of asceticism. I suggest as an example, the image of nakedness in John of the Cross, an image that lends itself to transformation.

"Nakedness" is a metaphor in the spiritual tradition for a condition in which one is stripped of selfish desires, and of the tendency to hang on or cling to anything that is not God. The mystics speak of the extreme pain of this experience and yet they also look upon it as an extraordinary gift of God. While the context and the concrete means that prepare one to stand naked before God differ significantly from medieval monasticism to late twentieth-century family life, I think our medieval sisters and brothers have something valuable to teach us.

In *The Ascent of Mount Carmel*, John uses the image of

nakedness to describe the entire process of what he calls "the dark night." He says, "We are presenting a substantial and solid doctrine for all those who desire to reach this nakedness of spirit."[6] The dark night includes various levels of being naked. The soul is stripped, both actively and passively, of sensible and spiritual appetites. First one becomes free of inordinate attachments to creaturely comforts like good food and fine clothing. Then one even ceases craving for spiritual comforts like consolation and feelings of intimacy with God.

> Hence, we call this nakedness a night for the soul. For we are not discussing the mere lack of things; this lack will not divest the soul, if it craves for all these objects. We are dealing with the denudation of the soul's appetites and gratifications; this is what leaves it free and empty of all things, even though it possesses them.[7]

What are the values at stake in John's portrayal of the denudation of the dark night?

For John, the stripping and the pain that accompanies the dark night are not objectives in themselves. Rather, the goal of the journey through the dark night is freedom. By purifying one's appetites, one becomes truly free to embrace God *and* all of God's creation. John counsels his sisters and brothers who have been called to the "narrow" way to denude themselves of everything but God for God's sake. To love means "to labor to divest and deprive oneself for God of all that is not God. When this is done the soul will be illumined by and transformed by God."[8]

John wishes his followers to be free from the kind of "wanting" that clings to things that are not God. Instead of being slaves or idolators, we become truly free to *enjoy* God, others, and the beauties of creation. This stripping is one aspect of a contemplative existence in which the Christian's life is characterized by a sense of gratitude for the giftedness of life. To be naked is to confront the "static" that blocks openness to, and communication with, God and others. For John, "contemplation is nothing but a secret, peaceful and loving inflow of God, which, if not hampered, fires the soul in the spirit of love."[9]

John's perceptive analysis of the human penchant to covet things of the world and the spirit is instructive, although we need to exercise care in appropriating his wisdom for our own time. John's experience of radical stripping took place in the sixteenth-century context of Carmelite monasticism. He was not a merchant, did not marry or raise children. But those of us whose lives are centered in the marketplace and within families are not thereby freed from the need to abandon covetous attitudes, and to engage in a "denuding" process. It is rather that we will experience this stripping in ways that are dramatically different from John's. Our initial positive attitudes toward nature, matter and the body cannot be compared with those of sixteenth-century Spanish monasticism. And yet each in her/his own time needs to let go of clinging ways in order to enter into the freedom of the children of God.

II. THE ASCETICISM OF EVERYDAY LIFE

While ascetic practices that one chooses can certainly be beneficial, there are dangers. We are familiar with the Reformation discussion of works/righteousness, and the danger inherent in attempting to win salvation through our own activity—performing ascetic practices in order to insure, through one's storehouse of grace, an eternal reward. This bank-account approach to the spiritual life violates one's sense of the utter graciousness of God toward us. An associated problem is the human tendency toward egoism. One becomes focused on the behavior, losing touch with its roots in love, and begins to assume a "better-than-thou" attitude toward others. Stories of extremely self-destructive asceticism lead us to ask questions about its authenticity and godliness.

But there is another way to think about asceticism, that is, the asceticism of everyday life. A wise friend once said to me, "You never need to go to Lent. Lent always comes to you." In other words, if we live even in a minimally conscious way, we cannot help but see that life brings most of us all kinds of opportunities for self-denial. Along this trajectory, one begins, not with fasting or abstinence, but with reverent attention to the "stuff" of our daily lives. When we focus too exclusively, as I think we have, on the old categories, we fail to see that the primary locus of asceticism is in our ordinary experience.

What are some concrete examples of the asceticism of everyday life? No doubt each person could marshall a lengthy list, since each life has its own unique contours and challenges. I mention four.

Simplicity of Life[10]

This first set of examples resembles traditional understandings of asceticism inasmuch as they are gestures that we initiate and choose. We not only confer meaning on these practices, but we also decide whether or not we will undertake them at all.

The first, and perhaps most obvious, opportunity for self-discipline lies in our urge toward consumerism. Signs of this disease include finding happiness, identity and self-worth in buying, collecting and having "things"; experiencing withdrawal symptoms when we are unable to acquire things for extended periods of time; having our most frequent and satisfying mode of recreation coincide with consumption of one kind or another.[11] We have seen how John of the Cross counsels against inordinate clinging to anything that is not God. This disposition is accompanied by a freedom that often leads us to pare down our possessions in a literal way as well. We can all find ways to simplify existence. In the musical suite, *Appalachian Spring,* American composer Aaron Copland, has made us familiar with the melody of an old Shaker melody, "The Gift to Be Simple."

> 'Tis the gift to be simple
> 'Tis the gift to be free
> 'Tis the gift to come down where we ought to be
> And when we find ourselves in a place just right
> 'Twill be in the valley of love and delight.
>
> When true simplicity is gained
> To bow and to bend we shan't be ashamed

To turn, turn, 'twill be our delight
'Til by turning, turning we come round right.

Mundane activities such as cleaning out attics, garages and basements or the more difficult decision to let the car sit in the driveway and take public transportation can be a start.

A corollary to reining in our consuming ways is the responsible and generous use of the wealth and the other resources we do possess. A simple lifestyle often results in added resources that we can contribute to the common good— whether that be by supporting institutions or the homeless. All of us are blessed in different ways with material, intellectual, physical and spiritual gifts. One can refuse to acknowledge gifts, squander them, or hoard them. The ascetic way calls us in the direction of servanthood—naming, celebrating and sharing generously and humbly what we have.

Preoccupation with health leads many Americans to practice disciplines in the areas of physical exercise, smoking, and food and alcohol consumption. While they might look the same on the surface, such practices can have quite contrary intentions. At one extreme is the person who is obsessed with self, with physical appearance or with the natural chemical "high" that running produces. At the other extreme is the person who consumes food and alcohol in moderation because she reverences her body as made in God's image.[12] Since God does not make "junk," one is under some obligation to care for the self as one of God's treasured creations. This individual practices a variety of disciplines, not because she is on an ego trip, but because she is conscious that part of her call as a Christian is to be a person "for others." Working on herself prepares her to be the best possible "self" to welcome others into her life. Being one's best self—physically, psychically and spiritually—can be a gracious gesture of deference to the "other."

Growing in popularity is behavior that takes seriously the dire threats to our ecosystem. These disciplines involve contributing time, energy, creativity and money to cleaning up and preserving the earth. In another vein, one can reflect on the wondrous gifts of clean air and water, developing attitudes and behaviors of reverence and careful use. Recycling paper, plastic, and metals is more than an annoyance, or following the law, or being "politically correct." Loving commitment to the ecological health of our planet can become a significant component of a truly contemplative lifestyle.

These and other similar disciplines have the potential not only to enhance our spiritualities, and our reverence for self, others, world and God, but often they contribute directly to the common good, to building up the body of Christ on earth. When spirituality was the exclusive domain of a small elite group in the church, there was much talk about voluntary poverty. Today when spirituality belongs to all the baptized, there is talk rather of a spirituality of frugality or voluntary simplicity.

This spirituality embodies a vision that can inspire us to work to change the world and a sense of tranquillity and profound joy in living a life that is not wasteful and cluttered with unnecessary possessions. The practice of an asceticism of simplicity can go a long way toward alleviating our frustration and paralysis in the face of the world's suffering. And even though it may not seem like much, it is a good place to begin. Changing our lifestyles symbolizes in a concrete way our commitment to change and to the possibility of another, better world. It also has the potential to affect others, nudging them by our example to question unexamined values and lifestyles.[13] We turn now to those opportunities for asceticism that are built into the very fabric of daily life.

Confronting Illusion

Life offers many opportunities to move from illusion to reality. Some illusions are inherited from culture, nation, or family. We see ourselves as better, more generous, or more intelligent than we really are. We may also cling to the illusion that we are not worth anything, or incapable of sustained good action. Other illusions are created as defense mechanisms of one kind or another. We have illusions about ourselves, about our children, about our situation in life, about friends, about God. In many situations the illusion is more favorable than the truth. In others, less so. In either case, they are false, and therefore incapable of serving as a foundation for building a loving and authentic life.

In general, we like our illusions. They are familiar and comfortable and we cling to them even though they lead to a dead end. We close our eyes when the truth intrudes on our picture, and we rarely seek outside perspectives from persons who might see more clearly than we do. Comments from other people that make us especially upset or angry often point to some part of the truth about ourselves we are not willing to face.

Asceticism of everyday life points to an alternative. In this form of asceticism we become more willing to undergo the necessary stripping, as the layers of illusion are peeled away. We engage in the discipline of seeking the truth about ourselves, of being on the watch for clues to the false dimensions of our lives. We become more open to let the old, self-centered self die, so that a new creation may emerge. Such an asceticism may involve the time and energy required to get at the truth of some political situation, local or global—and the action one must take as a result of knowing the truth. At other times, it may mean facing up to the growing chasm between true inner feelings and dispositions, and the self that is presented to others. It may mean watching attentively for the signals that others send us about the blocks to truth we have set up in our work and relationships. Such a process entails pain and suffering, but can lead to new life.

Aging and Death

A third example of everyday asceticism is the universal experience of aging and death. We might add here the experience of illness, great and small, suffered by many. For most, this opportunity first knocks in middle age. One's energy level and body functions begin to decline. The options are to cling ferociously to youth or to see our physical diminishment, and the mental strain that can accompany it, as part of a larger picture in which suffering and limitation become channels for coredemption and participation in Christ's sufferings—gestures of acceptance that nurture love and life in ourselves and others.

This letting-go intensifies when death approaches. For the elderly and seriously ill, the stripping can be intense—physical movement, eyesight, hearing, memory—even speech, slip out of one's control. How vulnerable we become—an opportunity to open ourselves ever more fully to the loving presence and care of God. In some ways, the practice of fasting, for example, pales in the light of this invitation to lay down one's life with courage and love.

The loved ones of the sick and elderly are invited to their own brand of asceticism. How do we deal with the fatigue and burnout of daily hospital visits? How do we manage to keep up the daily round of responsibilities that do not abate because someone in the family is ill or dying? How do we allow God to share the burden of grief and of the letting-go when a friend, child, or spouse dies? The weight of such experiences can crush us, or be seen as a call to lay down our lives in love, to open ourselves to the consoling grace of God's love, and emerge as persons fully alive in the Spirit.

This way of embracing life's trials as integral to spiritual growth does not support the idea that suffering is "good for us" and therefore good in itself. On the contrary, suffering, pain, and loss are to be fought at every turn. We are called to work tirelessly to eliminate the innocent suffering that inevitably accompanies war, greed, famine, poverty, and the tearing of our social fabric. Rather, this way looks to the pain and suffering that inevitably accompanies human existence, in order to gaze at this suffering in a new way. It invites us to use these stripping experiences as stepping stones to holiness rather than to deny them or to focus on less significant ways to engage in a sacrifice of our own choosing.

In the past, we have looked too exclusively to unusual ascetic models and have failed to see the heroism all around us. Even a visionary person such as Thomas Merton, the Cistercian monk of Gethsemane (d. 1968) can, on occasion, seem to miss the more ordinary examples of everyday asceticism. In a short piece in the *New Yorker,* Marvin Barrett offers a vivid description of the trauma of heart attack and cancer, and of life in the intensive care unit. He concludes, "Merton writes about the marginal man, the monk, the displaced person, the prisoner, those who live in the presence of death and go beyond it to become 'witness to life.' Why does he leave the other experts off his list—the old, the desperately ill?"[14]

Parenting

Another example is one experienced by a great number of people—raising children. In our society, the challenge of raising children is perhaps the ascetic opportunity *par excellence.* This is not to deny the profound joys and rewards of parenting—the unexpected gesture of love and gratitude (from a simple flower to a homemade birthday card); participating in the process of children's maturation; watching them and helping them to become loving persons; witnessing as they accomplish their goals, grow in learning and self-reflection.

But whether one has children or is simply helping or observing others raise them, one cannot but be struck by the minefield facing most parents today. How do we love children well? How do we allow them to become who they are meant to be, free from our excessive attempts to mold them into something else? How do we trust them? How do we expose them to values? How do we cope with alcohol, drugs, misuse of sexuality, indifference, selfishness, boredom, consumerism, etc., etc.? How do we let them go gracefully and lovingly, when the time comes?

Parents get a lot of bad press in the media. For the most part, parents have deep desires to love their children well, and they suffer untold agonies—both in the discernment as to how to raise their children, and in the experience of some failure that is an inevitable part of the process. Child-rearing is almost always an invitation to heroic asceticism.

It is not hard to find concrete examples, illustrative of the daily round of self-sacrifice that is the lot of most parents. Who does not recognize the rigors of car-pooling, of getting carloads of your own and others' children to school, to soccer games, to piano lessons, to science fairs? Young couples who must both be employed face hard decisions about child care. Single, working parents are stretched to their limit when children are sick or in need of extended periods of attention. A full night's sleep, time to oneself, the freedom to come and go as one pleases—all this must be given up, and given up in a way that is quite different from the monk who chooses to rise once or twice during the night to recite his prayers.

Huge chunks of life are laid down at the behest of infants. Later, parents must let go, allowing children to create their own futures in freedom. Who has not agonized over children who become victims of drug abuse, who lose all interest in learning, or who enter into other patterns of self-destructive behavior? What parent has not felt helpless after exhausting every possible mode of action without success? Suffering with children often perdures into the second and even third generations, with grandparents and great-grandparents continuing to be deeply involved in the lives of their families.

Conclusion

The ascetic life will look differently in poor or war-torn countries than it does in affluent or peaceful nations. It will be different for women and men, for persons of various ages, colors, belief systems and economic status.

This vision of asceticism is also overtly communal in its orientation. Authentic, private ascetic practices do redound to the welfare of the community, but a true asceticism of everyday life, by its very nature, directly enhances our life *together*. In either case—and the one does not exclude the other—the fruit is the same: tender compassion, freedom, joy, courage, and the fullness of life.

A theology of incarnation demands that we understand the role of asceticism in the spiritual life in terms of life's everyday demands and struggles. We are invited to reflect on our suffering and sacrifice in the light of the cross, the symbol of God's love for humanity and to participate in that love. Authentic asceticism furthers the kingdom of heaven on earth, contributing to a world in which justice and peace become the legacy shared by all. In following this "way," we can hope to experience life's challenges in a "grace-full" way and experience the gospel maxim about the lightness of God's burden. Asceticism also demands freedom. Often, we have little control over the sufferings that life brings, but we do have something to say about how we will respond. One response leads to the fullness of life; another to a life of anger, resentment, cynicism and despair.

The ascetic way is a part of one's total spirituality that includes a desire for God, an openness to the gifts God offers us, a willingness to learn about and confront the patterns of sinfulness in our lives. True asceticism is nurtured by a loving, attentive, contemplative stance toward the persons in our lives, by a willingness to "cross over" and walk in another's shoes, a desire to be patient and to commit to the long haul.

But what a shame if we would miss these daily invitations to heroic asceticism, to self-denial, to the free and loving surrender of life for another, and think that choosing to fast one day a month is the only avenue of asceticism available to us! As you did to the least of my brothers and sisters, you did to me (Mt 25:40). The spiritual life is a journey into the fullness of life and love in God and in one another. Traditional ascetic practice is one means that can be used to this end. However, I suggest that the asceticism of everyday life is the primary means available to Christians on their journey toward union with God in love.

It is time for the Christian community to make a paradigmatic shift of images. The model of asceticism for the Christian community can no longer be the emaciated, celibate monk with the sad, sallow face. The struggle of the loving, selfless parent can be a model for all of us, whether we are physical parents or not. As church, we are called to become more aware of the loving asceticism of everyday life. Only then will we be able to appreciate the heroic death to self that surrounds us, celebrate the presence of God in these forms of self-sacrifice, affirm, encourage and console one another, and look to the best of them as models in our own search for a life-filled existence.

NOTES

1. See Margaret Miles, *Fullness of Life: Historical Foundations for a New Asceticism* (Philadelphia: Westminster Press, 1981); Karl Rahner, "New Asceticism" in *The Practice of Faith* (New York: Crossroad, 1983); the entire issue of *Weavings* 6(Nov.–Dec. 1988).

2. Murchu, Diarmuid O. "Early Christian Asceticism and its Relevance Today," *Irish Theological Quarterly* 50 (1983–84): 86.

3. Margaret Miles, "The Recovery of Asceticism," *Commonweal* 110 (January 28, 1983): 40.

4. See volume in Paulist Press series, The Classics of Western Spirituality: Athanasius, *The Life of Antony and the Letter to Marcellinus* (1991).

5. Murchu, "Early Christian Asceticism," p. 83.

6. John of the Cross, *The Ascent of Mount Carmel,* Prologue, 8.

7. Ibid., I.3.4.

8. Ibid., II.2.5.7.

9. John of the Cross, *The Dark Night,* I.10.6.

10. See Duane Elgin, *Voluntary Simplicity: An Ecological Lifestyle that Promotes Personal and Social Renewal* (New York: Bantam, 1982).

11. Two recent fictionalized treatments of obsession with collecting are Susan Sontag, *The Volcano Lover* (New York: Farrar Straus Giroux, 1992); and T. Coraghessan Boyle, "Filthy With Things," *The New Yorker* (February 15, 1993), p. 76.

12. See Frances Moore Lappe, *Diet for a Small Planet* (New York: Ballantine, 1982) and *Food First: Beyond the Myth of Scarcity,* with Joseph Collins (New York: Ballantine, 1979).

13. Donal Dorr, *Spirituality and Justice* (Maryknoll, NY: Orbis, 1984), p. 142-43.

14. Marvin Barrett, "A Kind of Dying," *The New Yorker* (October 12, 1987): 40–43.

10

Contemplation: A Loving Gaze at the World

As we move toward new ways of understanding the spiritual life in broader, inclusive and more global terms, we are led to question traditional patterns of prayer and contemplation. If we believe that each baptized person is a potential saint, then contemplation has to have a central role in our everyday lives.

In the past, we have often understood action and contemplation in private and hierarchical ways. To a great extent, contemplation was associated with the canonically religious and clerical ways of life, while the active life was seen as the lot of the lay community that makes up the overwhelming majority of the church. Further, there was little doubt about which of these two ways was the superior, more direct, and more divine path. We can all recall scores of homilies on Mary and Martha that prove this point! The result, as we have seen, is an elitism in the spiritual life—an elitism in disharmony with the distinctly inclusive message of the New Testament.

These two paths have usually been defined in terms of one's stance toward the world. Actives were "in" it and contemplatives fled "from" it into monastic enclosure, reinforcing the now familiar polarities—secular/sacred; matter/spirit; profane/holy; lay/religious. This understanding of action and contemplation has adversely affected many in the church, but none more than the lay community. As a result, many lay persons exclude themselves *a priori* from the contemplative life and do not notice the potential for religious meaning in the activities which make up most of their day.

150

I. THE ROOTS OF OUR UNDERSTANDING

In 1948, T. Camelot described the subject of action and contemplation in the Christian tradition as both delicate and burning.[1] He also raised a question we are asking again today as we look anew to the sources of Christianity. Since the New Testament speaks neither of "contemplation" nor of the "contemplative life," why is it necessary to discuss it at all?

Christianity's Hebrew ancestry is certainly not marked by flight from the world or from matter. Israel's experience of the divine brought renewed effort to act justly in the world. It is a commonplace that the roots of the distinction between action and contemplation go back to the Greek world into which Christianity spread. Plato most clearly formulated the concepts of the active and contemplative ways as two distinct lifestyles that were mutually incompatible. The contemplative life was that lived by the philosopher, one untainted by the concerns of the world.[2] Aristotle viewed the tension between action and contemplation as that between the human and the divine. The philosopher was, in a sense, an alien—one who strove to be above the human in order to partake of the divine.

In the New Testament period, the strong eschatological emphasis and the Christian community's perception of the reigning political forces as enemies, caused a shift away from involvement with the body politic to more narrow individual and ecclesial concerns. Church and state, sacred and secular became pitted against each other.

The qualities of the two ways and the values attached to each took on new meaning when they were incorporated into Christianity. The fathers of the church struggled with the meaning of action and contemplation, and the rise of monasticism provided the occasion for a new identification of the terms. Contemplation became almost exclusively associated with those living a vowed monastic life. In turn, the active life was seen as a preliminary and lesser stage in the monastic journey to holiness.

Martin A. Hyatt studies this theme in John Chrysostom's (d. 407) *Treatise on the Priesthood.*[3] Chrysostom's goal in this text is to enhance the dignity of the priestly office and to defend himself against the charge of worldly ambition. For him, the priesthood is the greatest proof of love for Christ.[4] By contrast, monks are surrounded by safeguards which make it easier to live a life of virtue. According to Chrysostom, the priest needs more virtue and purity because of the active nature of his work in the world, exemplified by exposure to the temptations of women![5] In this treatise, members of the larger, lay Christian community do not merit discussion except that "they are entangled in worldly cares which render them more slothful in application to spiritual things."[6] This failure of the laity makes the priest's task even more difficult, demanding that he work harder (than monks) in his striving for perfection.

In the medieval period, the active life referred in part to the mendicant Franciscan and Dominican orders that were engaged in an active apostolate beyond the cloister. Lay persons did participate in third orders but were always seen as ancillary to the first and second orders.

Although many scientific and philosophical positions since the Middle Ages have sought to reverse the earlier tradition by rejecting contemplation and elevating action to the higher position;[7] and although individuals such as Luther and Ignatius of Loyola[8] did much to integrate the two; and in spite of our American penchant for activity and pragmatism, I believe we continue to struggle with the difficulties engendered by past understandings of the active and contemplative lives. Within Christian, and in particular within Roman Catholic communities, there remains a tendency to look at the spiritual life in terms of a hierarchy of value from top to bottom, with contemplation at the top and somehow opposed to action. This view has nurtured the idea that the contemplative (monastic) life is better and more pleasing to God than a life lived in action in the world. One often hears exhortations to active Christians not to lose sight of the contemplative dimension of their lives, but rarely have contemplatives been warned about forgetting to remain active for the good of the world.

II. RECENT LITERATURE

A survey of writing on action and contemplation in the last decade or so gives clues about how we are framing the question.[9] Many general treatments of spirituality include a section on contemplation, while fewer treat the relationship between action and contemplation.[10]

Some authors examine the theme of action/contemplation in specific texts. This kind of detailed research contributes admirably to our understanding of past meanings of action and contemplation.[11]

A second category of essays includes broader treatments of action and contemplation, arguing that they are not really distinct realities and that it is inaccurate to set them up in opposition to one another.[12] Several authors argue that love is the unifying force, being both the essence of contemplation and the dynamism of apostolic activity. All active relationships with others are modes of contemplation, since contemplative consciousness is simply the fullness of love.

A third group of articles take action for justice as their primary focus.[13] Models are those who willingly give up solitude to immerse themselves in the heart of human suffering.

There are also psychological analyses of action and contemplation. One author speaks of the mature personality as one that expresses itself in both action and contemplation, and questions whether any culture that exclusively emphasizes one or the other can be a healthy environment for human growth.[14]

Two articles, written in 1984 and 1985, may be described as personal testimony to the call to contemplation by active lay women.[15] Both see their calls as unusual, pointing indirectly to that aspect of the tradition which would see contemplation and "ordinary life" as unlikely partners. I describe their accounts at greater length since they exemplify one form of the problem we address in this chapter.

Kathy Mariani Smith describes herself as "a laywoman, married, the mother of two active teen-agers."[16] The article focuses on contemplation more than on action and the author points especially to the two hours she is able to carve out of each day—hours in which she takes the phone off the hook and enters into silence and solitude. Her perception of the enormity of the problems in today's world leads her to see discouragement and despair as an inevitable component of the active life unless action is grounded in prayer. The contemplative call is to receptivity, to hope, to openness, to the formation of Christ in us by the Holy Spirit.[17]

Carol Carstens is married, the mother of twin sons, and a professed sister in the Secular Franciscan Order. On one level, she offers a more integrated vision of action and contemplation than does Smith. For her, silence can be found in noise just as joy can be found in the cross. "For the lay contemplative, deep stillness is found in activity itself."[18] Contemplation should be measured by quality of presence not quantity of time in meditation.[19]

However, when she offers concrete examples of the contemplative life, she narrows her focus considerably. She images the contemplative environment as one without television and strongly resembling a monastery. She says: "Ideally the work place should be within walking distance of the home with worship occurring within that same work/home community. A kind of secular monastery is the university environment where one can reside, work, and worship within a defined community."[20] One might justifiably ask to what extent this serene scene describes the life of most busy Christians! While both women take steps toward integrating action and contemplation, the old divisions seem still to hold sway.

From this brief survey, we can see the great diversity of perspectives in the treatment of action and contemplation in contemporary life. The challenge of a spirituality of everyday life is to maintain the crucial importance of moments of solitary silence and being alone with God, without giving up on the possibility that we can also be contemplatives *in the midst* of the noise, the hubbub and the intense activity of our days.

III. NEW PERSPECTIVES

Given the laity's growing sense of the universal, baptismal call to holiness, their need to take seriously, and be responsible for, the contemplative aspect of life continues to demand attention. What are some fresh ways of viewing action and contemplation that will take into account our present experiences and values?

There are at least two ways to think about action and contemplation. The first refers to the overt life rhythms of motion/activity and rest/quiet. Life would be impossible without them. We are conscious during the day and rest in sleep at night. We work during the week and relax on weekends. We go away on vacations or "get-away" weekends in order to renew ourselves by changing our environment. Even though we may tend in a superficial way to glorify the restful pole and denigrate the necessity of work, both poles have value. One can quickly arrive at a new appreciation of work by contemplating or experiencing, as is the case with so many Americans, its absence.

In the spiritual life, one also experiences these rhythms. Overtly religious examples of contemplative moments might include Sunday liturgy, Bible study, private prayer, spiritual reading or retreats of one kind or another. For some Christians, time away on retreat is an indispensable component of a healthy spiritual life. And one can only hope that participation in such contemplative moments is encouraged and made possible for all those who seek them.

For others, the quiet moment must be stolen from pressing responsibilities that engulf one's day. Even in the busiest of lives, one needs to find time to slow down, to reflect, to ask about the meaning of all the activity, the larger context in which it makes sense and from which one discovers anew the motivation to keep at it in love. Plato's famous words ring down through the centuries: "The unexamined life is not worth living."

But there is another approach, one which attempts to see the seeds of contemplation *within* action itself. Such "noisy contemplation" holds primacy of place in the Christian community by dint of its very inclusiveness. This kind of contemplation, fueled by desire and practice, can become an integral part of anyone's life—like breathing. The point is not to set "noisy contemplation" over against more traditional ideas about the contemplative life. Moments apart, silence, solitude will never outgrow their usefulness in the spiritual life and indeed, they flow directly toward and away from a more engaged experience of contemplation.

By calling attention to "noisy contemplation" one hopes to

alert persons who are already experts in this way of living to recognize the connection between their lives and what the church has always taught about the holiness of the contemplative life. We are surrounded by contemplatives in action, but because of our categories we have failed to recognize them and have failed to call them by their proper name. This anonymity has been a deprivation to the community which receives life from the celebration of the "holy ones" in its midst. Such a discussion is also an invitation to every Christian to experience the universal call to holiness which is also a call to the heights of contemplative existence.

One of the most perceptive, creative and forward looking thinkers on this subject is William Callahan.[21] He too, sees a need for a shift in our images of prayer and religious faith. The monastic ideal emphasized the "love of God" aspect of the great commandment. Today we are called to a vision of life in which "love of neighbor" is primary and involvement with the earth is not a distraction, but the very core of our journey.

Using Jesus as model—one who led a basically active life, withdrawing only before major decisions—Callahan proposes a contemplative stance, posture, gaze, which attentively regards oneself, the other and the world. He, too, acknowledges that there will be times when going apart is necessary and important, but for the most part, faith nourishment will be found in the contemplative bonding we experience in the God present in the people and events of our daily living.

Beholding the world with a contemplative heart will be: a) built on life experience; b) simple; c) strong and durable; d) deep and loving; e) socially conscious; and f) hospitable. We have emphasized the importance of experience in the spiritual life. In this context, one proposes as a starting point, not past structures of monastic, contemplative existence, but rather an invitation to reflect on the ways in which we actually experience God in our daily lives. Callahan begins with a group of stories of "ordinary" persons, describing the joys and struggles of life as they perceive it. In order to appropriate this fresh perspective, many of us will have to "shelve" our preconceived notions of the meaning of contemplation—since these can block our own reflective processes—and ask ourselves: Can we identify contemplative moments, moments in which we were drawn near to God or felt particularly aware of the presence of God in self and others? Such reflection can be the beginning of identifying ways in which we already experience the contemplative way.

Becoming familiar with the "geography" of one's contemplative existence leads one to a range of curiosities. Some persons will begin to ponder the lack of a contemplative stance in their lives. Others, who discover how often they live in a contemplative way, may wonder about other contemplatives—both contemporary and past—and about how they spoke about and nurtured their contemplation. Still others will celebrate the quiet joy of the contemplative gift that has been offered and accepted in their lives.

The contemplative life is a life of simplicity. Such a life has to be available to anyone who seriously desires to follow the Lord. Callahan notes the importance of a "portable" contemplation and opposes it to deluxe "Airstream camper" spirituality.

> It must be simple enough to be smuggled into prison cells, comfort people who grieve alone, and pass between people who have nothing but love to share.[22]

We must be careful not to confuse simplicity with simplemindedness. True simplicity is always aware of, and embedded in, the immense complexities of existence. But it is not burdened by a long list of often unattainable prerequisites, such as spiritual direction, extended periods of silence, sophisticated prayer skills, lots of leisure, serenity and tranquillity. Noisy contemplation is available to us in the diverse and often challenging settings of life, settings that often include frustration, poverty, lack of education, tension, anxiety and insecurities of all kinds.

Contemplation must also be strong and durable. As we face the suffering of our world, we are not helped by spiritualities that encourage fragility, timidity, fear or flight. One thinks of the faithful support of friend for friend in sickness and trouble; of the fidelity of parents toward their children, and spouses toward each other in good times and bad; of the perseverance of those who struggle to alleviate suffering and right wrongs encountered along the way. This call to contemplation is offered freely and must be responded to freely. It is our choice to allow the compassionate grace of God to lift our fears and heal our anxious ways.

True contemplation is radical and loving. Callahan reminds us of the element of radicality in the Christian call to contemplation. The biblical record reveals an "all-or-nothing" element in Jesus and his followers. Jesus did not take the "safe" way out, but responded openly and honestly to those around him. It is a quality that in the early church was known as "purity of heart." Today we might refer to such persons as "one-track-ers"—persons who have a vision and who pursue that vision with passionate commitment. There is a wholeness or a totality about the contemplative life that is available to everyone who has the courage to respond affirmatively.

Perhaps more than ever before, we realize that contemplation must be broadly socially conscious. We have spoken at length about the role of the global village in any contemporary spirituality.

> We are to open our hearts to our brothers and sisters throughout the world...If our prayer is sound, it must empower and nurture such love in the hearts of people who follow Jesus.[23]

Action on behalf of justice and participation in the transformation of the world is a constitutive element of the gospel message. This does not mean that one puts aside a personal spirituality. But an authentic spirituality will lead from personal conversion, to loving attention to those near and dear to us, and on to a profound concern for all peoples and for the cosmos itself. This loving care cannot be forced or called forth on demand. Rather, it emerges at different rates for different people, surely and confidently opening hearts to embrace ever wider horizons with the love of God in Christ Jesus.

Finally, contemplation is hospitable. Hospitality is the ability to be welcoming and can be exercised on many levels. To begin, one may need to learn to be hospitable to oneself. One struggles to become the best possible person one can be, not as an ego trip, but because we owe our best selves *to the other.*

Hospitality can be offered to anyone we meet; to family members; to friends; to the sick and dying; to refugees; to coworkers. Often hospitality takes the form of shelter, food and drink. The dining room table can become a place of welcome and open hearts—the source and mirror of the more formal eucharistic banquet. Hospitality is a commanding metaphor, shaping our understanding of the contemplative life in the midst of a full and busy existence.

Parker Palmer, a well-known Quaker, offers another creative approach to the action/contemplation paradox.[24] Reflecting on the ups and downs of his own search for a contemplative existence, he understands contemplation as that event that draws one closer to God and to others. Along with Callahan, Palmer is convinced that silence and withdrawal cannot be the only, or even the primary, way to be contemplative. Palmer uses the metaphor "tug of war" to describe the experience of persons caught between the monastic vision of life and life in a world of action. Many of us think we should be more "contemplative," and when we are not (which is most of the time) we feel guilty, abandon the spiritual quest altogether, or feel diminished. The trick is to transform our concepts of action/contemplation and then live in creative tension between the poles of the paradox.

Palmer acknowledges that the spiritual renaissance of the last thirty years has been profoundly shaped by monastic metaphors such as silence, solitude, centeredness.[25] But he discovered, in his quest for those values, that the fit between the monastic vision and life in the world of action is not always a good one. If one is called to the world of action (as most of us are), these monastic metaphors can "disenfranchise the soul, for they tend to devalue the energies of active life rather than encourage us to move with those energies toward wholeness."[26]

Palmer sees action and contemplation, not as contradictory ideas, but as poles that must be held in tension. We must try to live the active/contemplative paradox authentically, but within that whole, we must also be faithful to the pole of our particular calling. The spiritual quest involves knowing the "rapture of being alive," and for most people, the path to that aliveness is called the active life.[27] For Palmer, action points to the ways in which we cocreate reality with others and with the Holy Spirit. Contemplation points to the ways in which we unveil illusion and move toward the truly real. When the fruit of action is the removal of illusion, then that act is contemplative.[28] Solitude is not simply physical isolation. Rather, it means being in possession of one's heart, one's identity, one's integrity.[29]

Noisy contemplation is contemplation that excludes no one. It challenges us to open our narrow categories of what we understand prayer to be and to realize that the command "to pray always" is eminently possible, indeed required for all of us. Contemplative praying is touching and being touched by the other in love. It is creative thought and work. It is living with reverent attention to, and gratitude for, every atom and act of creation.

It is visible in the simple acknowledgment when someone enters a room; in partners who gaze at one another in love; in parents who take a moment to look fondly at and appreciate their children; in people who face themselves honestly; who take responsibility for their lives and their gifts; who put in an honest day's work; who perceive injustice and work to alleviate it. "We follow Jesus when we deal lovingly with our own personal existence."[30]

The way to contemplation is not meant to be overwhelming and therefore, discouraging. One begins by *wanting* it. One is free to choose in the simple, ordinary setting of daily life to open one's heart. Such openness has the potential to transform our daily existence. "Such a habit of prayer can call forth beauty and love from what seems daily, ordinary, even ugly."[31] Jesus did not set us up for chronic failure, but for success in prayer, in our efforts to be loving contemplatives. What may begin with taking a moment to smell the roses can evolve into a life of profound contemplative joy and commitment to self, to others, to our God, and above all to our suffering world.

NOTES

1. "Action et contemplation dans la tradition chrétienne," *Vie spirituelle* 78 (1948): 272–301.

2. See Dom Cuthbert Butler, *Western Mysticism* (London: Constable & Co. Ltd., 1922), pp. 258–263; Nicholas Lobkowicz, *Theory and Practice: History of a Concept from Aristotle to Marx* (New York: University Press of America, 1967).

3. "The Active and Contemplative Life in St. John Chrysostom's Treatise on the Priesthood." *Diakonia* 15 (1980): 185–192.

4. Ibid., p. 185.

5. *De sacerdotio* VI, 2, 3.

6. Ibid., VI, 4.

7. In the essay cited earlier, Robert Bellah mentions precursors such as the Florentine civic humanists, Salutati and Bruni, who gave greater religious dignity to the active life; Machiavelli, Thomas Hobbes, Francis Bacon and the American pragmatists, who exalt the active life and in some sense abandon contemplation.

8. Richard Hauser's *Moving in the Spirit: Becoming A Contemplative in Action* (New York: Paulist Press, 1986), offers a practical guide to living in the Spirit, based almost exclusively on elements in the *Exercises* of Ignatius of Loyola.

9. Examples include Thomas Merton who dealt continually with the themes of action and contemplation. See *Conjectures of a Guilty Bystander* (Garden City: Doubleday & Co., 1966) and *Contemplation in a World of Action* (Garden City: Doubleday & Co., 1973). Tilden Edwards discusses action and contemplation under the rubric of "Sabbath rest." See *Sabbath Time* (New York: Seabury Press, 1982); *Spiritual Friend*, Ch. 4, "The Eternal Rhythms" (New York: Paulist Press, 1980); and "The Way to A Sound Eye," in *Living with Apocalypse* (San Francisco: Harper & Row, 1984), pp. 1–12. In *Christian Spirituality: Beginnings and Development* (Chicago: Loyola University Press, 1984), George Lane offers an extremely abbreviated historical survey of spirituality and suggests—I think too simplistically—that Ignatius of Loyola "solved" the problem of action and contemplation present in the earlier tradition. A recent treatment of a major Ignatian theme can be found in Avery Brooks' *Finding God in the World: Reflections on a Spiritual Journey* (San Francisco: Harper & Row, 1989).

10. A computer search on "contemplation" produces over a thousand entries. Couple "contemplation" with "action" and the yield is six.

11. J.P.H. Clark, "Action and Contemplation in Walter Hilton," *Downside Review* 97 (October 1979): 258–274.

12. Wayne Teasdale, "Contemplation and Action," *Homiletic and Pastoral Review* 83 (June 1983): 61–67; Thomas Charles Oddo, "The

Monk and the Activist: A Comparative Study of the Spirituality of Thomas Merton and Daniel Berrigan." Ph.D. dissertation, Harvard University, 1979.

13. Charity Keolsch, "Mary and Contemplation in the Marketplace," *Sisters Today* 54(June/July 1983): 594–597; William Callahan, "Spirituality and Justice: An Evolving Vision of the Great Commandment," in *Contemporary Spirituality: Responding to the Divine Initiative,* ed. Francis A. Eigo (Villanova, PA: Villanova University Press, 1983), pp. 137–161.

14. Robert Bellah, "To Kill and Survive or To Die and Become: The Active Life and the Contemplative Life as Ways of Being Adult." In *Adulthood.* ed. E. H. Erikson (New York: W.W. Norton & Co. Inc., 1978), pp. 61–80. Bellah sees recent activity in Roman Catholicism as contributing to the demise of the contemplative life: "The Catholic turn toward the world in the twentieth-century, in an effort to make the Jesuit model the model for the church as a whole, has further endangered the contemplative life by weakening one of the last lines of its defense." 76.

15. Carol Carstens, "Confession of a Lay Contemplative," *Spiritual Life* 30 (Winter 1984): 219–222: Kathy Mariani Smith, "Hope in the Midst of the Ordinary," *Spiritual Life* 31 (Summer, 1985): 71–74.

16. Smith, p. 71.

17. Ibid., p. 73.

18. Carstens, p. 221.

19. Ibid., p. 222.

20. Ibid., p. 221.

21. William Callahan, *Noisy Contemplation* (Washington, D.C.: Quixote Center, 1982). Callahan has also written a subsequent article, "Noisy Contemplation: Prayer in a Busy Life," *New Theology Review* 2(May 1989): 29–39.

22. *Noisy Contemplation,* p. 7.

23. Ibid., p. 8.

24. Parker Palmer, *The Active Life* (San Francisco: Harper & Row, 1990).

25. Palmer, *The Active Life,* p. 1.

26. Ibid., p.2.

27. Ibid., pp.7–9.

28. Ibid., p. 17.

29. Ibid., p. 28.

30. Callahan, pp. 9–10.

31. Ibid., p. 11.

11

The Liturgies of Culture and Cosmos

I. WIDENING CIRCLES OF COMMUNITY

A concern of contemporary theology and spirituality in North America is the recovery of the communitarian emphases in the tradition. Many are responding to what is perceived as a distorted emphasis on the individual.[1] Arguments that place community as the primordial human reality are cogent. Proponents contend that the "I" never stands alone, but is always qualified by social factors. The very act of conception is a communal experience, and we spend the first nine months of our existence in an incredibly intimate, symbiotic relationship in the womb. The "I" that slowly comes forth into consciousness is the result of constant interraction with others within family and then beyond it.

In his book, *Community and Disunity: Symbols of Grace and Sin,*[2] Jerome Theisen chooses community as the primary symbol of graced reality. He says:

> The divine favor that we call grace is ultimately directed to the formation of a community: a community of people on this earth, a community of believers in Jesus Christ, a community of the dead and newly alive in the presence of the loving God. Community is the ultimate favor of God. Theologically the word community functions as a verbal symbol of the goal of all divine giving and human striving.[3]

It is obvious that the number and kinds of community are legion, and all the communities to which we belong provide a part of the context for becoming saints.

Vatican II has opened our eyes to the value of culture. Our growing ecological consciousness has broadened the horizons of community to include the entire cosmos. While the faith community is indispensable as a context for the spiritual life, we now include culture as another important setting. And the broadest—one might say the primordial setting—for the spiritual life is the cosmos. All other expressions of community must be viewed and understood within this cosmic horizon. Past viewpoints that saw the faith community as the exclusive locus of God's activity no longer serve us. The faith community is crucial inasmuch as it is the place where God's universal generosity is explicitly named and celebrated. But we must not allow this truth to obscure God's all-embracing presence and activity in our graced world. Gregory Baum puts it well:

> While God's universal will to save and the universality of sufficient grace were acknowledged in all theological treatises, these themes never entered into the center of theological reflection, and so never modified the Christian approach to the world or became an essential part of the Church's preaching. In general, the teaching of the Church as well as her legislation and practice gave expression to the sharp division between the Church as the fellowship of grace and the world as the place of God's absence.[4]

As we will see below, a recovery of the wisdom literature as a biblical source that celebrates the achievements of culture is a step in the direction suggested by Baum. Because we have not always taken proper care to distinguish between "the world" and "sin," we have often found ourselves, as Christians, with a "we-they" mentality, that is, as believers, we see ourselves as having a corner on the market of grace, and *over against* the world.

The first order of business for us as everyday saints is to see ourselves as believers who are deeply at one with, and involved in, the wider world community. It is only from *inside* this wider community that we are able truly to see the fullness of the God-given gracefulness of the universe. This new vision will include the awareness that God's presence is everywhere around us in places like scientists' laboratories and union halls;

at dining room tables and in school rooms; in hospital rooms and hospices; and in ecological and feminist movements, many of which are not motivated by an explicit belief in God.

The perspective from which we can most legitimately raise a critical voice, point to sin, and call to renewal of life, is *inside* the wider social community. From the inside, one realizes that sin is not "out there" but within every person and in the many communities to which we belong. Rosemary Haughton addresses this issue in terms of God's judgment. She says:

> The Church itself can only be the community of the Spirit by knowing that it is the community of the world, and continuing to work, as worldly, under judgment.[5]

The Christian community which is and has to be worldly, knows itself under judgment and is therefore repentant and reconciled. By undergoing this act of God's judgment, the community exists as a spiritual community that, in turn, enables it not only to *be* God's judgment, but also to *utter* God's judgment on the world, which includes its own worldly existence. As soon as the church regards its task as *not* subject to judgment, it is guilty of blasphemy by rejecting God's judgments and condemning itself.[6]

Similarly, Jesus was free to criticize the Jewish community harshly, because he was a Jew. He was speaking from inside that community, motivated by love and a profound desire for its well-being. He took for himself no privileged place in terms of an exclusive hold on God's graciousness.

Being awake to the possibility of becoming a saint right where we find ourselves will depend, as we have seen, on awareness and on one's structures of meaning.[7] We have noted that one way to describe this awareness is "sacramental." The persons and events of daily life take on many meanings. One sees God operative within the structures of everyday living and nothing, a priori, can be excluded. We are free to see God's presence showered upon us in the moments of our day—or not at all.

We return now to treat in more detail the issues of culture and cosmos raised in chapter 4. Are there biblical and theological foundations that legitimate talk about the liturgies of culture and cosmos?

II. WISDOM CELEBRATES THE GOODNESS OF CULTURE

In a provocative book published in 1971, Walter Brueggemann called attention to a neglected part of the biblical tradition—Wisdom—that affirms the world, celebrates culture and affirms human responsibility and capability.[8] In the broad culture of which Israel was a part, literature that dealt with the quest for the meaning of life has been called "wisdom literature." These writings date back as far as the Egyptian Pyramid Age (c.2600–2175 B.C.E.). In the post-exilic period, influenced by the wisdom literature of her neighbors, Israel composed most of her wisdom literature which includes Proverbs, Ecclesiastes, The Song of Songs, Job, Ecclesiasticus, the Wisdom of Solomon and parts of the Psalms. Recent biblical scholarship suggests that the genre of wisdom is not limited to these books, but in fact is found throughout the Old Testament texts.

Brueggemann suggests that the major features of wisdom theology stand in direct contradiction to, and therefore challenge those aspects of church that are culture-fearing and culture-negating. He addresses his own reformed Protestant tradition, to the extent that they are "despisers of culture," but I think all Christians can be enlightened by his message. He says:

> The wise in Israel characteristically appreciate life, love life, value it, and enjoy it. They appropriate the best learning, newest knowledge, and most ingenious cultural achievements.[9]

Let us view four of the qualities Brueggemann attributes to this the wisdom literature.[10]

1. Wisdom believes that the goal and meaning of human existence is *life*. The instructions of Proverbs are designed to provide guidance on how to create and maintain life in all its fullness, not just longevity but emotional, physical, psychical,

social and spiritual assets. The term "life" is a metaphor for all the good and valuable things that persons hope for and work for in their daily lives. Roland Murphy calls "life" the kerygma of the book of Proverbs.[11]

> He who heeds instruction is on the path to life, but he who rejects reproof goes astray (Prov 10:17).

And again,

> The fear of the Lord prolongs life but the years of the wicked will be short (Prov 10:27).

The life which Wisdom sees as the goal and meaning of existence is neither extrinsic to the historical process nor solitary but applies to the well-being of the community and of each person within it *now*, in the present moment.

2. Wisdom affirms that the authority for life can be discerned in the common experience of the community. What is right and good is not decided by some office or individual person or institution, but only by the community's patient, careful discernment of what it ought to be doing to be fully human. From one perspective, this viewpoint is utilitarian. Behavior is recommended because it "works."

> Liberality is good and ought to be practiced because it makes a man wealthy (Prov 11:25).

> Graciousness is commended because the gracious person is honored (Prov 11:16).

> Diligence is endorsed because it brings a person effectiveness and influence (Prov 12:24).

> Tranquillity, as we are so slow to learn, gives a person bodily health (Prov 14:30).

These maxims are not merely common sense, but bold affirmations about life, a confession of faith that rejects the contrary view as being false and illegitimate. The statements are an invitation to "try it and see." Their validity rests upon the fact that life really happens this way. Church structures that dictate from above what is good for the community—without recourse to the community—become increasingly dysfunctional. In the context of wisdom, our moral failure is not resistance to authority, but our dullness, our wanting others to make decisions for us; our settling for old rules or easy guides; our assumption that life will come in some other way than by our willingness to choose it and pay up. Wisdom lets no one off the hook by facile reference to human or divine authority.

3. Wisdom affirms that persons have the primary responsibility for their destiny. It believes that the choices one makes and the fidelities one honors have an effect on destiny. It trusts that persons are capable of choosing wisely and deciding responsibly. Wisdom sees human beings in their strength, in their courage to function for the welfare of the community.

Death and life are in the power of the tongue (Prov 18:21).

He who pursues righteousness and kindness will find life and honor (Prov 21:21).

A righteous person falls seven times, and rises again; but the wicked are overthrown by calamity (Prov 24:16).

The mood of wisdom is not coercion but an affirmative summons for persons to recognize the tremendous opportunities that lie before them. Wisdom says that persons must exercise their humanness through responsible decision-making. Persons are viewed as come-of-age in a world from which the gods have fled. Persons are charged with overseeing the affairs of the world in freedom and intelligent attention to what needs to be done in the here and now. Wisdom does not emphasize the fallen, stupid, inept, sinful person, thereby providing a needed complement to theologies that see the human person primarily or exclusively in that light. Wisdom teaches that being human is an exalted role from which much is expected.

4. Finally, wisdom celebrates human capability in reference to the natural and social environment. Creation is viewed as a

good, healthy place to live, ordered by God and source of enjoyment and gratitude. Wisdom thinks resolutely within the framework of a theology of creation—a fact that takes on new and ominous contours in our present ecological situation. Wisdom calls us to reflect on the splendor, order, beauty and goodness of creation, and to be accountable to our responsibility to maintain and celebrate the life-giving capability of creation. A theology that focuses too exclusively on Christ as *savior* of sinners requires an orientation that takes a dim view of the world, a low view of the human person and rejects cultural achievement. A sapiential outlook does not minimize our need for Christ as savior, but it calls attention as well to our need for a Christ who is the fruition of the divine purpose for mature and capable stewardship and discipleship, a fruition in which we are called to participate.

To sum up, wisdom sees the human person as a trusted, valued creature in God's assessment, and by extension, the community should trust and value the human person. Wisdom values human enterprise and eschews viewing grace as an escape from the exigencies, joys and sorrows of earthly life. Wisdom also avoids the trap of making special claims for the faith community *at the expense* of the human community. The temptation to imperialism is overcome in the conviction that the fullness of new life is available to all.

The goals of wisdom are intimately connected with the goals of the human community—goals with which we are familiar because we live as members of that community. The goals of faith can never stand in contradiction to the goals of people for responsible, loving human community. One must criticize the presence of sin, but always from a stance within culture. The wisdom tradition calls us to renew our commitment to life and to our power and responsibility to work to make that life a reality.

This sapiential outlook challenges us to see our daily lives as the primary locus of the holy. The reverence and value assigned to human existence in this view lead us to a new appreciation of, and confidence in, the ordinary workings of the wider world. In the midst of enormous suffering and aggression across the globe, the wisdom tradition can help us trust in our ability and responsibility to discern and choose the good for ourselves and for the world.

There is a sacredness that lies deep within nature, persons and cosmos. Daily life is a sacred, worldly arena in which liturgy is celebrated. It is the activity in this sacred space that gives meaning to the formal liturgy we celebrate within the four walls of a church on Sunday. And it is this daily, primordial liturgy that Sunday liturgy supports and renews. To this "cosmic" liturgy we now turn.

III. THE COSMIC LITURGY

As Catholic Christians, we believe that embedded deep within all being, God's grace orients all of reality toward Godself. The Trinity, composed of distinct persons bound together in mutual respect, harmony and love, is reflected in the cosmos. The graced love of God expresses itself in the myriad forms of creation. The natural world has long been a source for our connection with, and imaging of, a gracious God. One can recall experiences in which one felt close to God and had an inkling of what God must be like—blazing sunsets, the composition of the petals on a rose, snow-capped peaks, roaring oceans or a desert in bloom.[12] Nature is a major influence on our image of God. One can also imagine how one's idea of God would be altered by a world of polluted air, dying vegetation and poisoned water. "If the water is polluted it can neither be drunk nor used for baptism, for it no longer bears the symbolism of life but of death."[13]

Some may object to proposing the cosmos as our primary community. The utter hugeness of it can be paralysing. But the experience of many persons today truly reflects a cosmic awareness. Landing on the moon, the continued growth of scientific knowledge about the world, fears about the destruction of the ozone layer and the rain forests, and about the growing number of extinct species—all this is part of contemporary experience.

The novelist and poet, John Updike, writes about recovering a deep sense of gratitude for the organic mechanisms that sustain us. In *Facing Nature,* there is a sequence of poems entitled "Seven Odes to Seven Natural Processes": Rot, Evaporation, Growth, Fragmentation, Entropy, Crystallization and Healing. For Updike, the otherness of nature, when rightly read, contains the signature of grace. In the ode on Healing, he says:

> A scab
> is a beautiful thing—a coin
> the body has minted, with an invisible motto:
> In God We Trust.[14]

Our kinship with nature is discerned by faith. Only a final trust can espy the graciousness of nature and enable us to receive its blessing. Thomas Berry reminds us that

> the natural world is the maternal source whence we emerge into being as earthlings. The natural world is the life-giving nourishment of our physical, emotional, aesthetic, moral and religious existence. The natural world is the larger sacred community to which we belong. To be alienated from this community is to become destitute in all that makes us human. To damage this community is to diminish our own existence.[15]

The horizon of the spiritual life is cosmic, containing within it the "ordinary" elements of holiness. It is here that we discover the true meaning of liturgy and sacrament.

In his article entitled "How to Receive a Sacrament and Mean It," Karl Rahner discusses the relationship between world and sacrament. He says:

> I propose a Copernican revolution in Catholic thinking about sacraments; instead of seeing in them a spiritual movement outward from the sacramental action of an effect in the world, we should look for a spiritual movement of the world toward the sacrament.[16]

Rahner exemplifies this principle with the eucharist, but states that the principle applies to all sacraments, except infant baptism because, in order to be operative, the principle requires a conscious faith not yet developed in an infant.

Rahner's thesis has been restated by the Dominican, Thomas O'Meara, who also speaks of the world/sacrament relationship in terms of a reversal. He says:

> The reversal is a move from symbol to reality, from church building to world, from liturgy to service. The reversal is affirming the liturgical side of ministry to be only one side of ministry—the symbol-sacramental side and source of ministry—and recognizing ministry to be more than liturgy, preaching more than preaching during the Eucharist, love more than the kiss of peace...Sacrament presumes reality...sacraments and worship were intended to confirm and nourish their ministries in the world.[17]

And in his book, *Gifts That Differ*, David Power says "...time seems to indicate that worship can only be true worship if it is part of a more broadly based community life. Hence the community, under its lay leadership, looks to matters of the temporal order, inclusive of mutual care within the community and of its responsibility in the social, political and cultural arenas."[18]

Rahner rehearses what average Catholics might feel at eucharist. They think of themselves as living in a profane world, bound by commandments that are hard to keep, yet called by God to an eternal reward. In order to get in touch with God, every now and then they step out of this profane world into a "fane," a holy place, where a true encounter with God is possible, where God appears not as commanding but as forgiving and strengthening. Having met God in the holy place, Christians return to the profane world, to their daily grind far from God. The sacrament alone puts them in touch with God and makes their lives "religious." In this view the eucharist is the real high point of Christian life.[19]

Rahner admits that this way of looking at the Christian life has some value, but that in fact it seems to be on the way out (this spoken twenty years ago!). He recognizes the difficulties involved in contemporary movements to desacralize Christianity, but admits that they reveal a high level of dissatisfaction with sacramental practice. He says, "It can be doubted whether even earnest Christians really experience the Mass as the high point of Christian life, as Vatican II called it."[20] Recent surveys amassing data on the religious experience of American Catholics confirm this judgment.

Sacraments become more meaningful to the extent that we become aware that the sacramental sign is the manifestation in one's own life and in the community of the grace that guides the history of the whole world. As believers, we are already part of the cosmic history of grace. Grace is present *everywhere* except where we have chosen to cut ourselves off from God.

In the past, we may have seen the sacraments as "discrete discharges of grace" into a profane world. But today our theology invites us to see the world as permanently graced at its root, borne up by God's self-communication *whether or not* we choose to accept it, *whether or not* our jaded sensibilities can perceive it. This vision of the cosmos happily undermines the unfortunate experience in which our religious lives and our "real" lives run parallel to each other and never meet. Instead, grace becomes the ultimate depth of everything we do in our daily, ordinary lives—birth, suffering, courage, failure, hope and death. Grace is the spiritual depth of everything we do when we realize ourselves in God's image—when we laugh, and cry, accept responsibility, love, live and die, stand up for truth, refuse to be self-preoccupied, serve our neighbors, hope against hope, cheerfully refuse to be embittered by the stupidity of daily life, keep silent not so that evil festers in the heart but so that it dies there—when, in a word, persons "live as they would like to live, in opposition to their selfishness and to the despair that always assails them. This is where grace occurs, because all this leads us into the infinity and victory that is God."[21]

For Christians, Jesus Christ is the fullest expression of this kind of grace, precisely in his ordinariness. He, too, lived, suffered, celebrated, hoped against hope and died. Grace is not only the sacred, depth dimension of everyday life, but it is also a power that binds us to one another and to God. In individual experience we discover the experiences of all, and in the living and dying of others, we discover ourselves.[22]

Sacraments, then, are the manifestation of the holiness

and redeemed status of the world. Rather than closing our-selves off from the world by entering a temple that walls off the Holy from the godless world outside, we need to proclaim that the Spirit is everywhere in the open expanse of God's world. Rahner laments the perpetual tragic misunderstanding that sees the sacramental sign, which should speak to us of the limit-lessness of God's grace, as an enclosure in which alone God and God's grace are to be found.

Rahner speaks dramatically of this cosmic liturgy. "The world and its history is the terrifying, sublime, death-and-immo-lation liturgy which God celebrates by the agency of humankind. The whole length and breadth of this monstrous history, full of superficiality, stupidity, insufficiency, and hatred on the one hand, and silent dedication, faithfulness unto death, joy, and sorrow on the other, constitutes the liturgy of the world, and the liturgy of Jesus on the cross is its culmination."[23] One function of liturgy is to present this stark truth again and again. Authentic eucharist proclaims that the liturgy of faith and the rightly lived history of the world are one and the same.

Rather than being the sole locus of the real world or adding something to the world, eucharist celebrates and laments what is truly happening in the world. We offer the world in bread and wine, conscious that the world is already offering itself in triumph and tears and blood to God. "We gaze into God's face knowing that the real vision is given to eyes blinded with tears or glassy with approaching death. We receive the body of the Lord authentically when we are in communion with *the* body of God, which is the world itself with its fate. We speak the word of God, aware that it is the verbal expression of the divine word which is the world and the Word in which God eternally says 'yes' to this world."[24]

In acknowledging the primordial liturgy of the cosmos, authentic celebration of eucharist helps us to renew our partici-pation in, and commitment to, that cosmic liturgy. In word, song and ritual, eucharist reminds us of the sacredness of the universe, and should, ultimately, help us to be cocreators of that sacredness. In turn, a renewed sense of the sacramentality of the everyday life of the cosmos cannot but enhance our partici-pation in, and understanding of, formal sacraments. In the past we have not fully understood the reciprocal flow between world and sacrament. Too often, we saw grace as a one-way street flowing from sacrament to the world. Today we understand formal sacraments in the context of the wider arena in which we live and undertake our part in the work of redemption.

Rahner reminds us that Christians do not need to think that when sacraments are celebrated, God does something God would not do if they were not celebrated. Rather, we must realize that sacraments spring from, express, and lead to, the divine depths of real life. We are growing in the realization that the experiences of God and grace in our daily lives are the selfsame experiences that are ritualized in worship. Formal liturgy is an important but "tiny sign" of the liturgy of the world.[25]

A theological recovery of the world involves a transformation of our ideas about liturgy. The primary theater of the spiritual life is ordinary, worldly existence. The opportunities for growth in the Spirit, indeed, for heroic sanctity, are available to all and are embedded in the very fabric of our glorious, mundane, agonizing, ecstatic, sin-filled, generous, humdrum, quotidian existence. Theology and ministry struggle to come to terms with these truths.

NOTES

1. Cf. Robert Bellah, et al. *Habits of the Heart: Individualism and Commitment in American Life* (San Francisco: Harper & Row, 1985).

2. Jerome P. Theisen, OSB. *Community and Disunity: Symbols of Grace and Sin* (Collegeville, MN: St. John's University Press, 1985).

3. Ibid., p. x.

4. Gregory Baum, *Man Becoming: God in Secular Language* (New York: Herder & Herder, 1970), p. 25.

5. Rosemary Haughton, *The Theology of Experience* (New York: Newman Press, 1972), p. 56.

6. Ibid., pp. 56–59.

7. The reader may want to refer to Part I, chapter 2 above to review what was said there about structures of meaning.

8. Walter Brueggemann, *In Man We Trust* (Atlanta: John Knox Press, 1972). This entire section relies heavily on Brueggemann's text.

9. Ibid., p. 14.

10. Ibid., pp. 14–28.

11. Roland Murphy, "The Kerygma of the Book of Proverbs," *Interpretation*, Vol. XX (January 1966): pp. 3–14. Cited in Brueggemann, p. 14.

12. In order to avoid a naive and overly romantic view of nature, one needs to take into account the violent, destructive aspects of nature as well. See Annie Dillard, *Pilgrim At Tinker Creek* (New York: Harper & Row, 1976).

13. Thomas Berry, "Economics as a Religious Issue," privately distributed paper, p. 12.

14. John Updike, *Facing Nature,* ed. Judith Jores (New York: Knopf, 1985), p. 84.

15. Thomas Berry, Ibid., p. 17.

16. Karl Rahner, "How to Receive A Sacrament and Mean It," *Theology Digest* 19(Autumn 1971): 227–234. I rely on Rahner's argument throughout this section.

17. Thomas O'Meara, *Theology of Ministry* (New York: Paulist Press, 1983), p. 199.

18. David Power, *Gifts That Differ: Lay Ministries Established and Unestablished* (New York: Pueblo Publishing Company, 1980), p. 29.

19. Rahner, Ibid., p. 227.

20. Ibid., p. 227.

21. Ibid., p. 228.

22. Ibid., p. 229.

23. Ibid., p. 229.

24. Ibid., p. 230.

25. Ibid., p. 30.

Conclusion:
All Is Grace

The concept of grace serves as an appropriate copestone for our discussion of the foundations and building blocks of a spirituality of everyday life, a spirituality that is the inheritance of all baptized Christians. In his massive christological study, *Christ*, Edward Schillebeeckx reassures us that communion with God through the Son in the Spirit is in fact a living communion that *can be experienced*.[1] And while the true contemplative experiences everything in life as gift, it is also true that expectations and confidence play very important roles. If we don't expect ourselves and others to become saints, in fact, it is not likely that we will. Unfortunately in the past, there was little expectation that lay persons would be the recipients of such graces. As a result, we have few lay models who are known and held up to the community. But these obstacles cannot, in the end, block the Spirit from working within our communities nor should they block us from recognizing and celebrating that presence.

This book has offered a viewpoint in which grace is understood as an open concept, capable of embracing the whole of God's self-gift to us, and thus, capable of indefinitely various further particularization. Leonardo Boff underscores this idea of grace.

> We can never talk about grace in itself because it shows up in this particular thing or that particular thing...Grace is not something isolated in itself that stands apart from other things. Grace is a mode of being that things take on when they come into contact with the love of God and are

suffused with [God's] mystery. In that sense the whole world is related to grace.[2]

Grace is a "mode of being" that is available to every baptized Christian. Every person, every reality in the cosmos is touched by God's love.

We can speak in a similar way about sin. It is not an isolated phenomenon, but a "mode of being" that things take on when we say no to the call to holiness. In John's first epistle, he tells us that if we say we have no sin, then we deceive ourselves and live in darkness (1 Jn 1:6–8). Sin is death, draining us of energy and life. Sin is refusal—saying no to love, to life's blessings and pleasures, no to relationship with God and other persons. Sin tempts us to remain as children, refusing to become responsible adults, or to develop our gifts fully. Irresponsible is the choice to limit oneself falsely, to think that the call to holiness, to heroic love, to a contemplative lifestyle is for *other* people. Sin is an attitude that takes creation for granted and ends up abusing it.

Sin is also the choice to live in illusion, to avoid the truth of existence, of gifts, of one's dark side. Many persons also experience sin as being trapped, tempted to despair, being held captive. Others speak of sin primarily in terms of fear—fear of self, of others, of taking risks, of speaking out. Such sin is the refusal to trust that God is good and that we are good because loved by God. This results in a life of excessive control, of hanging on, of clinging to self, to others, of grasping for love or life or material things. Sin is giving in to self-hate and to the insecurity that results in a life whose main focus is self-protection at the expense of others. Finally, sin is visible in the cold heart that supports a life of indifference, of apathy, a life devoid of passion and gratitude. We can live life as though life "owed" us, or we can live life aware of its utter giftedness in every detail—a life characterized by thanks and praise. This is the life that is visible in the saints and this is the life to which we are called as everyday saints.

As our circle of discourse broadens to include persons of color, women, children, the elderly, persons from other religions, we can be assured that the multiplicity of voices will enhance the celebration of the height, depth, length and breadth of God's glory, God's unbounded graciousness to every creature.

The message of all this talk about becoming "everyday saints" can be boiled down to this simple phrase: "All is grace." The Judeo-Christian tradition portrays a God with many faces. But one of those faces is a God whose existence is fulfilled in communicating God's very self in love, to us creatures. The fourteenth-century anchoress, Julian of Norwich reports that God said to her, "See, I am God. See, I am in all things. See, I do all things. See, I never remove my hands from my works, nor ever shall without end."[3]

The experience of grace is human experience. The cosmos, human life, and history are the loci of this self-communication of God. The experience of grace is also *real*. It is not pseudo-experience or experience that runs parallel to one's genuine concerns and values. To discover where one's heart is, is to discover the hub of grace's activity—or its absence. Grace takes on a thousand different faces for women and men, rich and poor, white and black, French and African. The unifying element is a generous loving God present to us as Spirit. The work of grace is totally God's and totally ours.

The community's ultimate test by which it judges a life of holiness is the fruit that it bears. We included no separate chapter on virtuous dispositions or action for justice, because these have been a leitmotif running through our entire discussion.[4] These fruits need to become visible in our self-understanding, in our relationships, in work, in the way we deal with suffering and sin, in the way we regard the universe and everyone and everything in it. These fruits are many. A sampling might include inner freedom, peace, courage in the face of suffering, willingness to act against injustice, truth-telling, kindness and compassion, and above all joy, hope, and gratitude.

Others before us have told us that grace is everywhere. And if grace is everywhere, then all of us can become everyday saints. This conviction takes on an added dimension when it is affirmed in the midst of physical, psychological and spiritual suffering. In a time and circumstance very different from our own, Thérèse of Lisieux (d. 1897), during the months of pain and suffering that preceded her death, notes, "Without a doubt, it's a great grace to receive the sacraments; but when God doesn't allow it, it's good just the same; everything is a grace."[5]

And the well-known twentieth-century French novelist, Georges Bernanos, writes of the life and ministry of a priest in rural France. The curé describes his parish as a place inflicted with the "leprosy of boredom: an aborted despair, a shameful form of despair in some way like the fermentation of a Christianity in decay." Yet in his diary he describes believers in the following way:

> A worldling can think out the pros and cons and sum up his chances. But what are *our* chances worth? We who have admitted once and for all into each moment of our puny lives the terrifying presence of God?[6]

At the end of the novel, the curé, who is now very ill, goes to visit a needy friend (a defrocked priest) in his dismal quarters, and there meets an obscure and inglorious death. His friend who had hastily called for a priest to administer the last rites later writes of the event.

> The priest was still on his way, and finally I was bound to voice my deep regret that such a delay threatened to deprive my comrade of the final consolation of the church...He then uttered these words...And I am quite sure that I have recorded them accurately, for his voice, though halting, was strangely distinct:

> "Does it matter? Grace is everywhere..."[7]

NOTES

1. Edward Schillebeeckx, *Christ: The Experience of Jesus as Lord.*

2. Leonardo Boff, *Liberating Grace,* trans. John Drury (Maryknoll, NY: Orbis Books, 1979), p. 28.

3. Julian of Norwich, *Showings* (New York: Paulist Press, 1978), chapter 11.

4. There are many books that focus on spirituality and justice.

Some suggestions include: Dietrich Bonhoeffer, *The Cost of Discipleship* (New York: Macmillan, 1963); Joe Donders, *Non-Bourgeois Theology: An African Experience of Jesus* (Maryknoll, NY: Orbis, 1985); Donal Dorr, *Spirituality and Justice* (Maryknoll, NY:Orbis Books, 1984); J. Gremillion, ed. *The Gospel of Peace and Justice* (Maryknoll, N.Y.: Orbis, 1976); Gustavo Gutierrez, *We Drink From Our Own Wells: The Spiritual Journey of A People,* trans. Matthew J. O'Connell (Maryknoll, NY: Orbis, 1984 [1983]); John C. Haughey, ed. *The Faith That Does Justice* (New York:Paulist Press, 1977); Abraham Heschel, *The Prophets* (New York: Harper & Row, 1962).

    5. Thérèse of Lisieux, *Her Last Conversations*, trans. John Clarke (Washington, D.C.: ICS Publications, 1977).

    6. Georges Bernanos. *Diary of a Country Priest* trans. Pamela Morris (Chicago: The Thomas More Press, 1983 [1937]), p. 5-6.

    7. Ibid., p. 298.

Index